Parrot Fire Kris Northern

"Rather than zoom into the fractal you can zoom into the edge of it and continually
find the same pattern repeating itself much like the shoreline of a lake viewed
from a plane." – **Kris Northern**

Student Math Handbook

Investigations
IN NUMBER, DATA, AND SPACE®

Editorial offices: Glenview, Illinois • Parsippany, New Jersey • New York, New York
Sales offices: Boston, Massachusetts • Duluth, Georgia
Glenview, Illinois • Coppell, Texas • Sacramento, California • Mesa, Arizona

The Investigations curriculum was developed by TERC, Cambridge, MA.

This material is based on work supported by the National Science Foundation ("NSF") under Grant No.ESI-0095450. Any opinions, findings, and conclusions or recommendations expressed in this material are those of the author(s) and do not necessarily reflect the views of the National Science Foundation.

ISBN: 0-328-24092-3

ISBN: 978-0-328-24092-0

20-V082-18 17 16 15 14

Math Words and Ideas

Number and Operations

Patterns, Functions, and Change

Data and Probability

Geometry

Measurement

Games

Games Chart 115

The **Student Math Handbook** is a reference book.
It has two sections.

Math Words and Ideas

These pages illustrate important math words and ideas that you have been learning about in math class. You can use these pages to think about or review a math topic. Important terms are identified and related problems are provided.

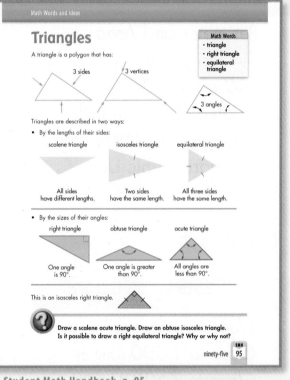

▲ Student Math Handbook, p. 95

Games

You can use the Games pages to go over game rules during class or at home. They also list the materials and recording sheets needed to play each game.

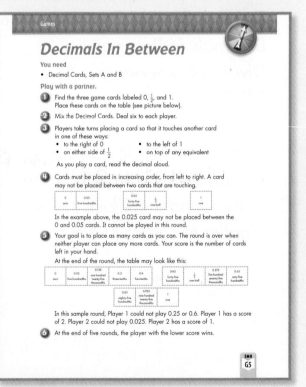

▲ Student Math Handbook, p. G5

Daily Practice and Homework pages list useful *Student Math Handbook* (SMH) pages.

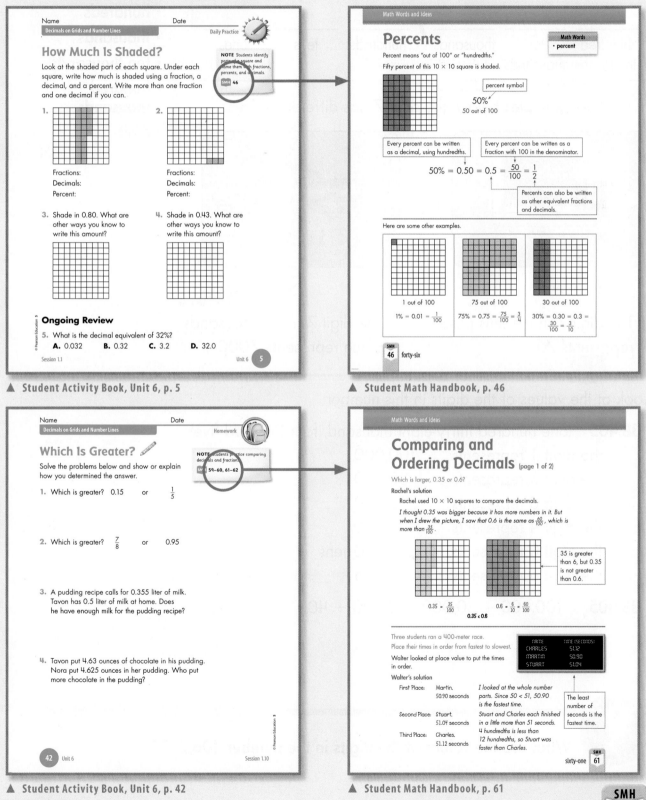

Page one (Student Activity Book, Unit 6, p. 5):

Name _____ Date _____

Decimals on Grids and Number Lines

Daily Practice

How Much Is Shaded?

Look at the shaded part of each square. Under each square, write how much is shaded using a fraction, a decimal, and a percent. Write more than one fraction and one decimal if you can.

NOTE Students identify parts of a square and name them with fractions, percents, and decimals.

SMH 46

1.

Fractions:
Decimals:
Percent:

2.

Fractions:
Decimals:
Percent:

3. Shade in 0.80. What are other ways you know to write this amount?

4. Shade in 0.43. What are other ways you know to write this amount?

Ongoing Review

5. What is the decimal equivalent of 32%?
   A. 0.032   **B.** 0.32   **C.** 3.2   **D.** 32.0

Session 1.1   Unit 6   5

© Pearson Education 5

▲ Student Activity Book, Unit 6, p. 5

Page two (Student Math Handbook, p. 46):

Math Words and Ideas

Percents

Math Words
• percent

Percent means "out of 100" or "hundredths."

Fifty percent of this 10 × 10 square is shaded.

percent symbol

50%

50 out of 100

Every percent can be written as a decimal, using hundredths.

Every percent can be written as a fraction with 100 in the denominator.

$$50\% = 0.50 = 0.5 = \frac{50}{100} = \frac{1}{2}$$

Percents can also be written as other equivalent fractions and decimals.

Here are some other examples.

| 1 out of 100 | 75 out of 100 | 30 out of 100 |

$1\% = 0.01 = \frac{1}{100}$ $75\% = 0.75 = \frac{75}{100} = \frac{3}{4}$ $30\% = 0.30 = 0.3 = \frac{30}{100} = \frac{3}{10}$

SMH
46 forty-six

▲ Student Math Handbook, p. 46

Page three (Student Activity Book, Unit 6, p. 42):

Name _____ Date _____

Decimals on Grids and Number Lines

Homework

Which Is Greater?

Solve the problems below and show or explain how you determined the answer.

NOTE Students practice comparing decimals and fractions.

SMH 59–60, 61–62

1. Which is greater?   0.15   or $\frac{1}{5}$

2. Which is greater? $\frac{7}{8}$ or   0.95

3. A pudding recipe calls for 0.355 liter of milk. Tavon has 0.5 liter of milk at home. Does he have enough milk for the pudding recipe?

4. Tavon put 4.63 ounces of chocolate in his pudding. Nora put 4.625 ounces in her pudding. Who put more chocolate in the pudding?

42 Unit 6   Session 1.10

© Pearson Education 5

▲ Student Activity Book, Unit 6, p. 42

Page four (Student Math Handbook, p. 61):

Math Words and Ideas

Comparing and Ordering Decimals (page 1 of 2)

Which is larger, 0.35 or 0.6?

Rachel's solution

Rachel used 10 × 10 squares to compare the decimals.

I thought 0.35 was bigger because it has more numbers in it. But when I drew the picture, I saw that 0.6 is the same as $\frac{60}{100}$, which is more than $\frac{35}{100}$.

35 is greater than 6, but 0.35 is not greater than 0.6.

$0.35 = \frac{35}{100}$ $0.6 = \frac{6}{10} = \frac{60}{100}$

0.35 < 0.6

Three students ran a 400-meter race.
Place their times in order from fastest to slowest.
Walter looked at place value to put the times in order.

NAME	TIME (SECONDS)
CHARLES	51.12
MARTIN	50.90
STUART	51.04

Walter's solution

First Place: Martin. 50.90 seconds

I looked at the whole number parts. Since 50 < 51, 50.90 is the fastest time.

Second Place: Stuart. 51.04 seconds

Stuart and Charles each finished in a little more than 51 seconds. 4 hundredths is less than 12 hundredths, so Stuart was faster than Charles.

Third Place: Charles. 51.12 seconds

The least number of seconds is the fastest time.

SMH
sixty-one 61

▲ Student Math Handbook, p. 61

Place Value

The value of a digit changes depending on its place in a number.

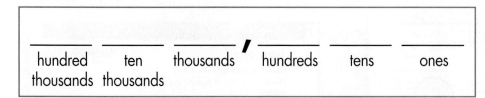

hundred thousands   ten thousands   thousands , hundreds   tens   ones

Math Words
- **place value**
- **ones**
- **tens**
- **hundreds**
- **thousands**
- **ten thousands**
- **hundred thousands**
- **digit**

In the two examples below, the digit 7 has different values.

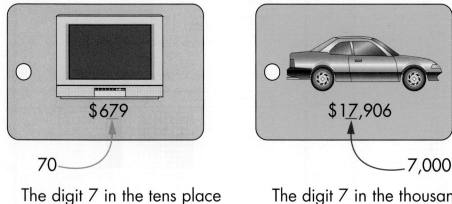

$679

70

$17,906

7,000

The digit 7 in the tens place represents 70.

The digit 7 in the thousands place represents 7,000.

Look at the values of the digits in this number:

138,405   (one hundred thirty-eight thousand, four hundred five)

the digit 1 represents	100,000
the digit 3 represents	30,000
the digit 8 represents	8,000
the digit 4 represents	400
the digit 0 represents	0 tens
the digit 5 represents	5

138,405 = 100,000 + 30,000 + 8,000 + 400 + 5

What are the values of the digits in the number 106,297?

Place Value of Large Numbers

Math Words
- **million**
- **billion**
- **trillion**
- **googol**

A pattern is used to name very large numbers.

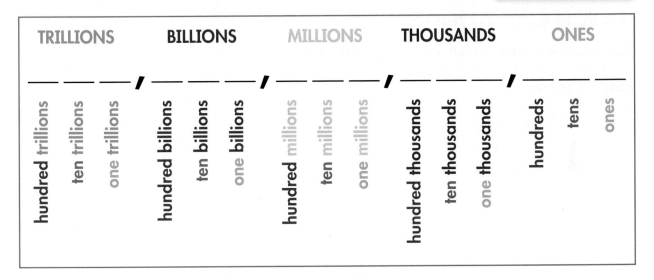

TRILLIONS			BILLIONS			MILLIONS			THOUSANDS			ONES		
hundred trillions	ten trillions	one trillions	hundred billions	ten billions	one billions	hundred millions	ten millions	one millions	hundred thousands	ten thousands	one thousands	hundreds	tens	ones

Every three digits are separated by a comma.
The three grouped digits share a name (such as "millions").

Within a group of three digits, there is a pattern of ones, tens, and hundreds.

Very large numbers are used to count heartbeats.

(one)		about 1 heartbeat per second
(one thousand)	1,000	heartbeats in less than 20 minutes
(one million)	1,000,000	heartbeats in less than 2 weeks
(one billion)	1,000,000,000	heartbeats in about 35 years

A googol is a very, very large number!

One googol is written as the digit 1 followed by 100 zeros.

10,000,000,000,000,000,000,000,000,000,000,000,000,
000,000,000,000,000,000,000,000,000,000,000,000,000,
000,000,000,000,000,000

Addition Strategies (page 1 of 2)

In Grade 5 you are practicing addition strategies.

$$6,831 + 1,897 =$$

Breaking Apart the Numbers

Rachel solved the problem by adding one number in parts.

Rachel's solution

```
    6,831
 + 1,000
    7,831
 +   800
    8,631
 +    90
    8,721
 +     7
    8,728
```

Charles, Zachary, and Janet solved the problem by adding by place.
Their solutions are similar, but they recorded their work differently.

Charles's solution	Zachary's solution	Janet's solution
6,831 + 1,897 =	6,831	¹ ¹
6,000 + 1,000 = 7,000	+ 1,897	6,831
800 + 800 = 1,600	7,000	+ 1,897
30 + 90 = 120	1,600	**8,728**
1 + 7 = 8	120	
8,728	8	
	8,728	

Addition Strategies (page 2 of 2)

6,831 + 1,897 =

Changing the Numbers

Cecilia solved the problem by changing one number and adjusting the sum. She changed 1,897 to 2,000 to make the problem easier to solve.

Cecilia's solution

$$
\begin{array}{r}
6,831 \\
+\ 2,000 \\
\hline
8,831 \\
-\quad 103 \\
\hline
\mathbf{8,728}
\end{array}
$$

I added 2,000 instead of 1,897.

Then I subtracted the extra 103.

Benito solved the problem by creating an equivalent problem.

Benito's solution

6,831 + 1,897 =
(−3)   (+3)   I added 3 to 1,897 and
subtracted 3 from 6,831.

6,828 + 1,900 = **8,728**

Show how you would solve the problem 6,831 + 1,897.

Subtraction Strategies (page 1 of 4)

In Grade 5, you are using different strategies to solve subtraction problems efficiently.

$$3,726$$
$$- 1,584$$

Subtracting in Parts

Tamira solved this problem by subtracting 1,584 in parts.

Tamira's solution

$$
\begin{array}{r}
3,726 \\
- 1,000 \\
\hline
2,726 \\
- 500 \\
\hline
2,226 \\
- 80 \\
\hline
2,146 \\
- 4 \\
\hline
\mathbf{2,142}
\end{array}
$$

> I started at 3,726 and jumped back 1,584 in four parts: 1,000, then 500, then 80, and then 4. I landed on 2,142. The answer is the place where I landed.

$3,726 - 1,584 = \mathbf{2,142}$

Subtraction Strategies (page 2 of 4)

$$3,726$$
$$-\ 1,584$$

Adding Up

Felix added up from 1,584.

Felix's solution

$$1,584\ +\ \underline{\hspace{1cm}}\ =\ 3,726$$
$$1,584\ +\ 2,000\ =\ 3,584$$
$$3,584\ +\ \ \ \ 116\ =\ 3,700$$
$$3,700\ +\ \ \ \ \underline{\ 26}\ =\ 3,726$$
$$\mathbf{2,142}$$

> The answer is the total of all the jumps from 1,584 up to 3,726.

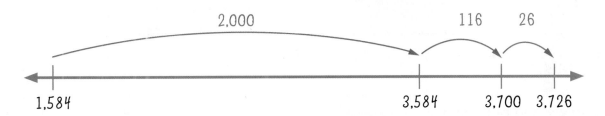

Subtracting Back

Walter used a subtracting back strategy.

Walter's solution

$$3,726\ -\ 1,584\ =\ \underline{\hspace{1cm}}$$
$$3,726\ -\ 2,126\ =\ 1,600$$
$$1,600\ -\ \ \ \underline{\ 16}\ =\ 1,584$$
$$\mathbf{2,142}$$

> The answer is the total of the two jumps from 3,726 back to 1,584.

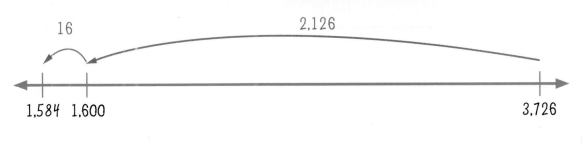

Subtraction Strategies (page 3 of 4)

$$3{,}726$$
$$- 1{,}584$$

Changing the Numbers

Hana solved the problem by changing one number and adjusting the answer.

Hana's solution

$$3{,}726 - 1{,}600 = 2{,}126$$
$$2{,}126 + 16 = \textbf{2{,}142}$$

> I subtracted 1,600 instead of 1,584. I subtracted too much, so I added 16 back on.

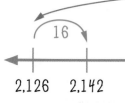

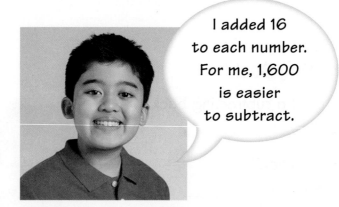

Joshua solved the problem by creating an equivalent problem.

Joshua's solution

$$3{,}726 - 1{,}584 =$$
$$(+16) \quad (+16)$$

$$3{,}742 - 1{,}600 = \textbf{2{,}142}$$

> I added 16 to each number. For me, 1,600 is easier to subtract.

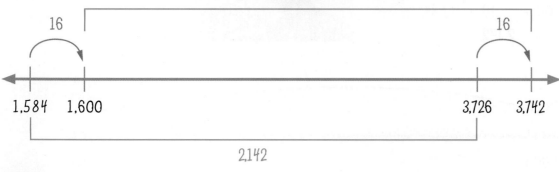

Subtraction Strategies (page 4 of 4)

$$3{,}726$$
$$-\ 1{,}584$$

Subtracting by Place

Yumiko subtracted by place. She combined positive and negative results to find her answer.

Yumiko's solution

$$3{,}726$$
$$-\ 1{,}584$$
$$2$$
$$-\ 60$$
$$200$$
$$2{,}000$$
$$\mathbf{2{,}142}$$

This notation shows each step in Yumiko's solution.

$$3{,}000\ +\ 700\ +\ 20\ +\ 6$$
$$-\ (\ 1{,}000\ +\ 500\ +\ 80\ +\ 4\ )$$
$$2{,}000\ +\ 200\ +\ -60\ +\ 2\ =\ \mathbf{2{,}142}$$

Avery subtracted by place, using the U.S. algorithm.

Avery's solution

$$3{,}\overset{6}{\cancel{7}}26$$
$$-\ 1{,}584$$
$$\mathbf{2{,}142}$$

This notation shows each step in Avery's solution.

$$3{,}000\ +\ \overset{600}{\cancel{700}}\ +\ \overset{100}{20}\ +\ 6$$
$$-\ (\ 1{,}000\ +\ 500\ +\ 80\ +\ 4\ )$$
$$2{,}000\ +\ 100\ +\ 40\ +\ 2\ =\ \mathbf{2{,}142}$$

 How would you solve the problem 3,726 – 1,584?

Multiplication and Division

> **Math Words**
> - **multiplication**
> - **division**

× Use multiplication when you want to combine groups that are the same size.

Number of groups	Size of group	Number in all the groups	
28 teams	18 players on each team	*unknown*	There are 28 youth soccer teams in our town, and there are 18 players on each team. How many players are there on all of the teams? $$28 \times 18 = \underline{504}$$ Answer: There are **504** players in all.

÷ Use division when you want to separate a quantity into equal-sized groups.

Number of groups	Size of group	Number in all the groups	
28 teams	*unknown*	504 players	There are 28 soccer teams in our town and 504 players altogether on all the teams. Each team has the same number of players. How many players are there on each team? $$504 \div 28 = \underline{18}$$ Answer: Each team has **18** players.

Number of groups	Size of group	Number in all the groups	
unknown	18 players on each team	504 players	There are 504 soccer players in our town, and there are 18 players on each team. How many teams are there? $$504 \div 18 = \underline{28}$$ Answer: There are **28** teams.

Mathematical Symbols and Notation

Multiplication

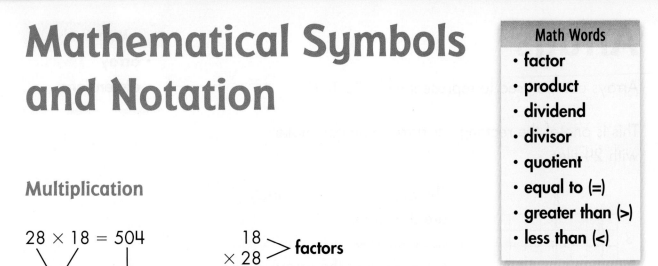

$28 \times 18 = 504$

factors product

$\begin{array}{r} 18 \\ \times\, 28 \\ \hline 504 \end{array}$ factors

504 — product

Division

$120 \div 15 = 8$

dividend divisor quotient

divisor quotient

$15\overline{)120}$

dividend

Comparing values

equal to	$2 \times 40 = 2 \times 5 \times 8$	$80 = 80$
greater than	$10 \times 10 > 11 \times 9$	$100 > 99$
less than	$4 \times 30 < 3 \times 50$	$120 < 150$

What are the factors in $14 \times 20 = 280$?

What is the quotient in $144 \div 16 = 9$?

Arrays

Arrays can be used to represent multiplication.

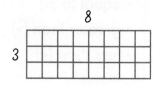

Math Words
- **array**
- **dimensions**

This is one of the rectangular arrays you can make with 24 tiles.

8

3

The dimensions of the array are 3 × 8 (or 8 × 3, depending on how you are looking at the array).

This array shows that

- 3 and 8 are two of the factors of 24.
- 24 is a multiple of 8.
- 24 is a multiple of 3.

This array shows a way to solve 8 × 12.

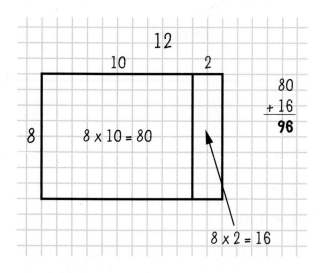

12

10   2

8   8 x 10 = 80

80
+ 16
96

8 x 2 = 16

8 × 12 = (8 × 10) + (8 × 2) = 80 + 16 = **96**

Draw an array with dimensions 5 by 9.

Unmarked Arrays

For larger numbers, arrays without grid lines can be easier to use than arrays with grid lines.

Look at how unmarked arrays are used to show different ways to solve the problem 9×12.

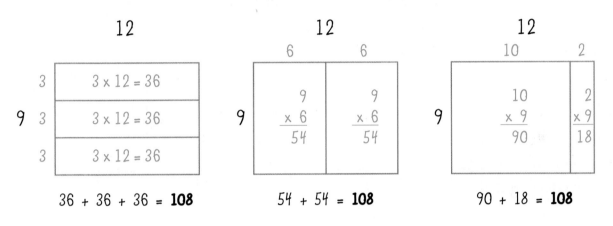

$36 + 36 + 36 = \mathbf{108}$ $54 + 54 = \mathbf{108}$ $90 + 18 = \mathbf{108}$

This unmarked array shows a solution for 34×45.

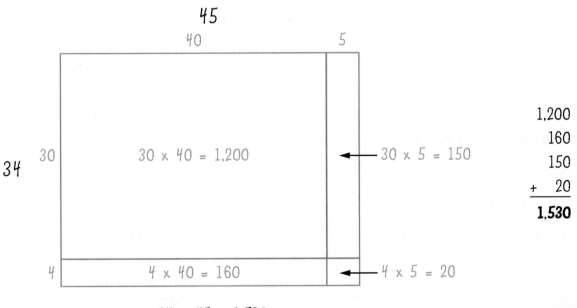

$34 \times 45 = \mathbf{1,530}$

Factors

Math Words
• factor

These are all the possible whole-number rectangular arrays for the number 36, using whole numbers.

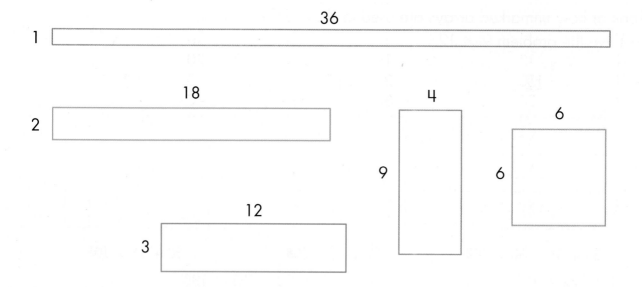

Each dimension of these rectangles is a factor of 36.

Listed in order, the factors of 36 are

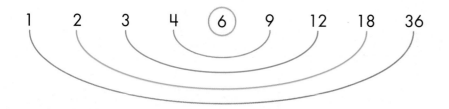

1   2   3   4   6   9   12   18   36

Pairs of factors can be multiplied to get a product of 36.

$1 \times 36 = 36$	$2 \times 18 = 36$	$3 \times 12 = 36$
$4 \times 9 = 36$	$6 \times 6 = 36$	$9 \times 4 = 36$
$12 \times 3 = 36$	$18 \times 2 = 36$	$36 \times 1 = 36$

Use the factors of 36 to find the factors of 72.
Use the factors of 36 to find the factors of 360.

Multiples

Math Words
• multiple

This 300 chart shows skip counting by 15. The shaded numbers are multiples of 15. A multiple of 15 is a number that can be divided evenly into groups of 15.

1	2	3	4	5	6	7	8	9	10
11	12	13	14	15	16	17	18	19	20
21	22	23	24	25	26	27	28	29	30
31	32	33	34	35	36	37	38	39	40
41	42	43	44	45	46	47	48	49	50
51	52	53	54	55	56	57	58	59	60
61	62	63	64	65	66	67	68	69	70
71	72	73	74	75	76	77	78	79	80
81	82	83	84	85	86	87	88	89	90
91	92	93	94	95	96	97	98	99	100
101	102	103	104	105	106	107	108	109	110
111	112	113	114	115	116	117	118	119	120
121	122	123	124	125	126	127	128	129	130
131	132	133	134	135	136	137	138	139	140
141	142	143	144	145	146	147	148	149	150
151	152	153	154	155	156	157	158	159	160
161	162	163	164	165	166	167	168	169	170
171	172	173	174	175	176	177	178	179	180
181	182	183	184	185	186	187	188	189	190
191	192	193	194	195	196	197	198	199	200
201	202	203	204	205	206	207	208	209	210
211	212	213	214	215	216	217	218	219	220
221	222	223	224	225	226	227	228	229	230
231	232	233	234	235	236	237	238	239	240
241	242	243	244	245	246	247	248	249	250
251	252	253	254	255	256	257	258	259	260
261	262	263	264	265	266	267	268	269	270
271	272	273	274	275	276	277	278	279	280
281	282	283	284	285	286	287	288	289	290
291	292	293	294	295	296	297	298	299	300

$\underline{20} \times 15 = 300$

$300 \div 15 = \underline{20}$

Use the shaded numbers on the 300 chart to write other multiplication and division equations about the multiples of 15.

$\underline{\quad?\quad} \times 15 = \underline{\quad?\quad} \qquad \underline{\quad?\quad} \div 15 = \underline{\quad?\quad}$

Multiple Towers

When you skip count by a certain number, you are finding multiples of that number.

Nora's class made a multiple tower for the number 16. They recorded the multiples of 16 on a paper strip, starting at the bottom.

They circled every 10th multiple of 16 and used them as landmark multiples to solve the following problems.

$\underline{\quad 21 \quad} \times 16 = 336$

Nora's solution

*We know that $20 \times 16 = 320$.
336 is next on the tower after 320,
so it is one more 16.*

$30 \times 16 = \underline{\quad 480 \quad}$

Georgia's solution

*30×16 would be the next
landmark multiple on our tower.
Since $3 \times 16 = 48$,
then $30 \times 16 = 48 \times 10$.*

$208 \div 16 = \underline{\quad 13 \quad}$

Renaldo's solution

*Ten 16s land on 160.
Three more 16s will go to 208.*

336
(320) 20 X 16
304
288
272
256
240
224
208
192
176
(160) 10 X 16
144
128
112
96
80
64
48
32
16

How would you use this multiple tower to solve this problem?
$18 \times 16 = \underline{\qquad}$

Properties of Numbers

(page 1 of 2)

Math Words
• **prime number**
• **composite number**
• **square number**

When a number is represented as an array, you can recognize some of the special properties of that number.

Prime numbers have exactly two factors: 1 and the number itself.

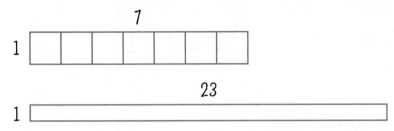

7 and 23 are examples of prime numbers.

Numbers that have more than two factors are called composite numbers.

The number 1 has only one factor. It is neither a prime number nor a composite number.

A square number is the result when a number is multiplied by itself.

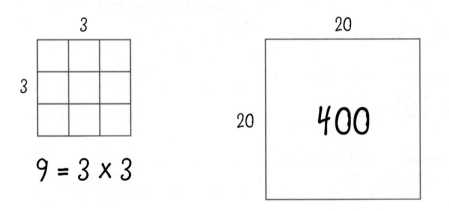

$$9 = 3 \times 3$$

9 and 400 are examples of square numbers.

Properties of Numbers
(page 2 of 2)

An even number is composed of groups of 2. One of the factors of an even number is 2.

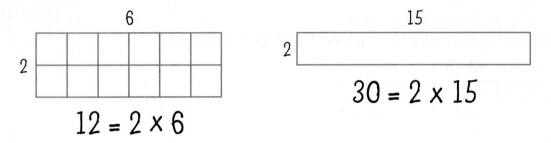

$$12 = 2 \times 6$$

$$30 = 2 \times 15$$

12 and 30 are examples of even numbers.

An odd number is composed of groups of 2 plus 1. An odd number does not have 2 as a factor.

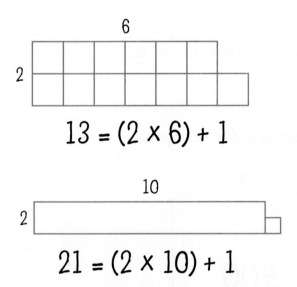

$$13 = (2 \times 6) + 1$$

$$21 = (2 \times 10) + 1$$

13 and 21 are examples of odd numbers.

Find all the prime numbers up to 50.
Find all the square numbers up to 100.

Multiplying More than Two Numbers (page 1 of 2)

There are 36 dots in this arrangement.

You can visualize the total number of dots in many ways.

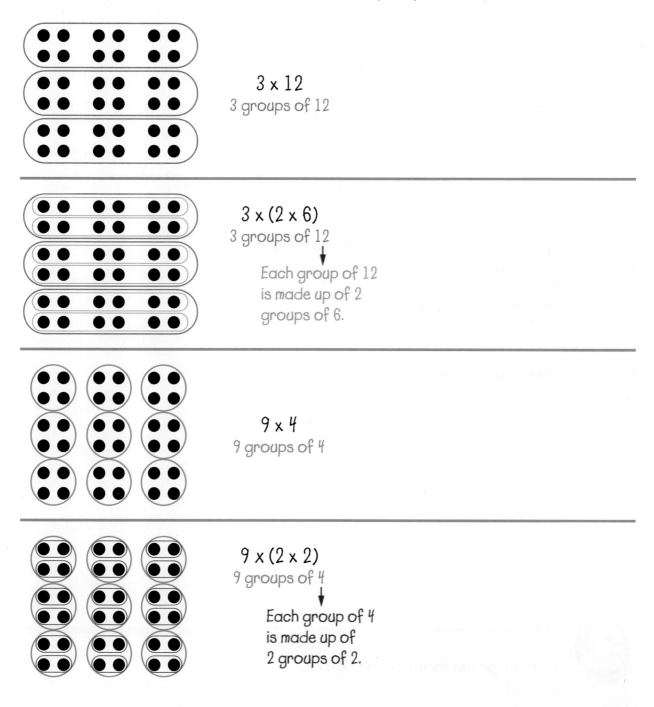

3 x 12
3 groups of 12

3 x (2 x 6)
3 groups of 12
↓
Each group of 12
is made up of 2
groups of 6.

9 x 4
9 groups of 4

9 x (2 x 2)
9 groups of 4
↓
Each group of 4
is made up of
2 groups of 2.

Multiplying More than Two Numbers (page 2 of 2)

Here are ways to multiply whole numbers to make 36.

two factors	three factors	four factors
2 x 18	2 x 2 x 9	2 x 2 x 3 x 3
3 x 12	2 x 3 x 6	
4 x 9	3 x 3 x 4	
6 x 6		

$2 \times 2 \times 3 \times 3$ is the longest multiplication expression with a product of 36 using only whole numbers greater than 1.

(2) x (2) x (3) x (3)

Notice that these factors are prime numbers.

$2 \times 2 \times 3 \times 3$ is the prime factorization of 36.

Find the prime factorization of 120.

Multiplication Combinations

(page 1 of 5)

One of your goals in math class this year is to review and practice all the multiplication combinations up to 12 × 12.

1 x 1	1 x 2	1 x 3	1 x 4	1 x 5	1 x 6	1 x 7	1 x 8	1 x 9	1 x 10	1 x 11	1 x 12
2 x 1	2 x 2	2 x 3	2 x 4	2 x 5	2 x 6	2 x 7	2 x 8	2 x 9	2 x 10	2 x 11	2 x 12
3 x 1	3 x 2	3 x 3	3 x 4	3 x 5	3 x 6	3 x 7	3 x 8	3 x 9	3 x 10	3 x 11	3 x 12
4 x 1	4 x 2	4 x 3	4 x 4	4 x 5	4 x 6	4 x 7	4 x 8	4 x 9	4 x 10	4 x 11	4 x 12
5 x 1	5 x 2	5 x 3	5 x 4	5 x 5	5 x 6	5 x 7	5 x 8	5 x 9	5 x 10	5 x 11	5 x 12
6 x 1	6 x 2	6 x 3	6 x 4	6 x 5	6 x 6	6 x 7	6 x 8	6 x 9	6 x 10	6 x 11	6 x 12
7 x 1	7 x 2	7 x 3	7 x 4	7 x 5	7 x 6	7 x 7	7 x 8	7 x 9	7 x 10	7 x 11	7 x 12
8 x 1	8 x 2	8 x 3	8 x 4	8 x 5	8 x 6	8 x 7	8 x 8	8 x 9	8 x 10	8 x 11	8 x 12
9 x 1	9 x 2	9 x 3	9 x 4	9 x 5	9 x 6	9 x 7	9 x 8	9 x 9	9 x 10	9 x 11	9 x 12
10 x 1	10 x 2	10 x 3	10 x 4	10 x 5	10 x 6	10 x 7	10 x 8	10 x 9	10 x 10	10 x 11	10 x 12
11 x 1	11 x 2	11 x 3	11 x 4	11 x 5	11 x 6	11 x 7	11 x 8	11 x 9	11 x 10	11 x 11	11 x 12
12 x 1	12 x 2	12 x 3	12 x 4	12 x 5	12 x 6	12 x 7	12 x 8	12 x 9	12 x 10	12 x 11	12 x 12

There are 144 multiplication combinations on this chart. You may think that remembering all of them is a challenge, but you should not worry. On the next few pages you will find some suggestions for learning many of them.

Multiplication Combinations

(page 2 of 5)

Learning Two Combinations at a Time

To help you review multiplication combinations, think about two combinations at a time, such as 8×3 and 3×8.

These two problems look different but have the same answer.

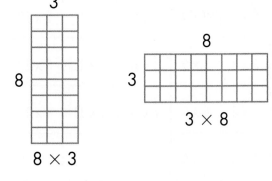

3

8

8×3

8

3

3×8

When you know that $8 \times 3 = 24$, you also know that $3 \times 8 = 24$.

You've learned two multiplication combinations!

By "turning around" combinations and learning them two at a time, the chart of multiplication combinations is reduced from 144 to 78 combinations to learn.

1 x 1	1 x 2	1 x 3	1 x 4	1 x 5	1 x 6	1 x 7	1 x 8	1 x 9	1 x 10	1 x 11	1 x 12
2 x 1 1 x 2	2 x 2	2 x 3	2 x 4	2 x 5	2 x 6	2 x 7	2 x 8	2 x 9	2 x 10	2 x 11	2 x 12
3 x 1 1 x 3	3 x 2 2 x 3	3 x 3	3 x 4	3 x 5	3 x 6	3 x 7	3 x 8	3 x 9	3 x 10	3 x 11	3 x 12
4 x 1 1 x 4	4 x 2 2 x 4	4 x 3 3 x 4	4 x 4	4 x 5	4 x 6	4 x 7	4 x 8	4 x 9	4 x 10	4 x 11	4 x 12
5 x 1 1 x 5	5 x 2 2 x 5	5 x 3 3 x 5	5 x 4 4 x 5	5 x 5	5 x 6	5 x 7	5 x 8	5 x 9	5 x 10	5 x 11	5 x 12
6 x 1 1 x 6	6 x 2 2 x 6	6 x 3 3 x 6	6 x 4 4 x 6	6 x 5 5 x 6	6 x 6	6 x 7	6 x 8	6 x 9	6 x 10	6 x 11	6 x 12
7 x 1 1 x 7	7 x 2 2 x 7	7 x 3 3 x 7	7 x 4 4 x 7	7 x 5 5 x 7	7 x 6 6 x 7	7 x 7	7 x 8	7 x 9	7 x 10	7 x 11	7 x 12
8 x 1 1 x 8	8 x 2 2 x 8	8 x 3 3 x 8	8 x 4 4 x 8	8 x 5 5 x 8	8 x 6 6 x 8	8 x 7 7 x 8	8 x 8	8 x 9	8 x 10	8 x 11	8 x 12
9 x 1 1 x 9	9 x 2 2 x 9	9 x 3 3 x 9	9 x 4 4 x 9	9 x 5 5 x 9	9 x 6 6 x 9	9 x 7 7 x 9	9 x 8 8 x 9	9 x 9	9 x 10	9 x 11	9 x 12
10 x 1 1 x 10	10 x 2 2 x 10	10 x 3 3 x 10	10 x 4 4 x 10	10 x 5 5 x 10	10 x 6 6 x 10	10 x 7 7 x 10	10 x 8 8 x 10	10 x 9 9 x 10	10 x 10	10 x 11	10 x 12
11 x 1 1 x 11	11 x 2 2 x 11	11 x 3 3 x 11	11 x 4 4 x 11	11 x 5 5 x 11	11 x 6 6 x 11	11 x 7 7 x 11	11 x 8 8 x 11	11 x 9 9 x 11	11 x 10 10 x 11	11 x 11	11 x 12
12 x 1 1 x 12	12 x 2 2 x 12	12 x 3 3 x 12	12 x 4 4 x 12	12 x 5 5 x 12	12 x 6 6 x 12	12 x 7 7 x 12	12 x 8 8 x 12	12 x 9 9 x 12	12 x 10 10 x 12	12 x 11 11 x 12	12 x 12

Multiplication Combinations

(page 3 of 5)

Another helpful way to learn multiplication combinations is to think about one category at a time. Here are some categories you may have seen before.

Learning the ×1 Combinations

You may be thinking about only one group.

1 group of 9 equals 9.

$\rightarrow$ 1 x 9 = 9

You may also be thinking about several groups of 1.

6 groups of 1 equal 6.

$\rightarrow$ 6 x 1 = 6

Learning the ×2 Combinations

Multiplying by 2 is the same as doubling a number.

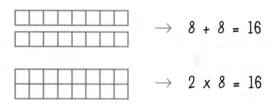

$\rightarrow$ 8 + 8 = 16

$\rightarrow$ 2 x 8 = 16

Learning the ×10 and ×5 Combinations

You can learn these combinations by skip counting by 10s and 5s.

10, 20, 30, 40, 50, 60 $\rightarrow$ 6 x 10 = 60

5, 10, 15, 20, 25, 30 $\rightarrow$ 6 x 5 = 30

Another way to find a ×5 combination is to remember that it is half of a ×10 combination.

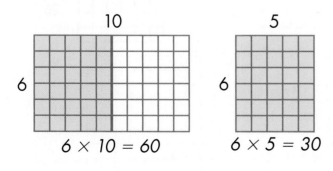

6 x 5 (or 30) is half of 6 x 10 (or 60).

Multiplication Combinations

(page 4 of 5)

Here are some more categories to help you learn the multiplication combinations.

Learning the ×11 Combinations

Many students learn these combinations by noticing the double-digit pattern they create.

$$\begin{array}{ccccc} 11 & 11 & 11 & 11 & 11 \\ \underline{\times 3} & \underline{\times 4} & \underline{\times 5} & \underline{\times 6} & \underline{\times 7} \\ 33 & 44 & 55 & 66 & 77 \end{array}$$

Learning the ×12 Combinations

Many students multiply by 12 by breaking the 12 into 10 and 2.

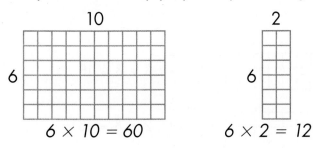

$6 \times 10 = 60$ $6 \times 2 = 12$

$6 \times 12 = (6 \times 10) + (6 \times 2)$
$6 \times 12 = 60 + 12$
$6 \times 12 = 72$

Learning the Square Numbers

Many students remember the square number combinations by building the squares with tiles or drawing them on grid paper.

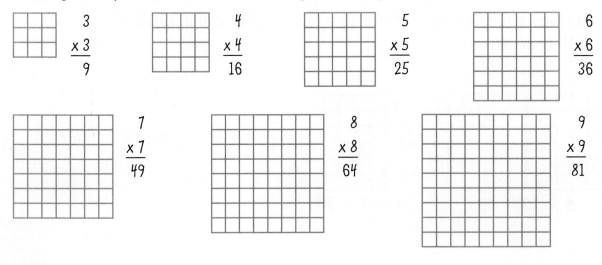

Multiplication Combinations

(page 5 of 5)

After you have used all these categories to practice the multiplication combinations, you have only a few more to learn.

1 x 1	1 x 2	1 x 3	1 x 4	1 x 5	1 x 6	1 x 7	1 x 8	1 x 9	1 x 10	1 x 11	1 x 12
2 x 1	2 x 2	2 x 3	2 x 4	2 x 5	2 x 6	2 x 7	2 x 8	2 x 9	2 x 10	2 x 11	2 x 12
3 x 1	3 x 2	3 x 3	3 x 4	3 x 5	3 x 6	3 x 7	3 x 8	3 x 9	3 x 10	3 x 11	3 x 12
4 x 1	4 x 2	4 x 3 3 x 4	4 x 4	4 x 5	4 x 6	4 x 7	4 x 8	4 x 9	4 x 10	4 x 11	4 x 12
5 x 1	5 x 2	5 x 3	5 x 4	5 x 5	5 x 6	5 x 7	5 x 8	5 x 9	5 x 10	5 x 11	5 x 12
6 x 1	6 x 2	6 x 3 3 x 6	6 x 4 4 x 6	6 x 5	6 x 6	6 x 7	6 x 8	6 x 9	6 x 10	6 x 11	6 x 12
7 x 1	7 x 2	7 x 3 3 x 7	7 x 4 4 x 7	7 x 5	7 x 6 6 x 7	7 x 7	7 x 8	7 x 9	7 x 10	7 x 11	7 x 12
8 x 1	8 x 2	8 x 3 3 x 8	8 x 4 4 x 8	8 x 5	8 x 6 6 x 8	8 x 7 7 x 8	8 x 8	8 x 9	8 x 10	8 x 11	8 x 12
9 x 1	9 x 2	9 x 3 3 x 9	9 x 4 4 x 9	9 x 5	9 x 6 6 x 9	9 x 7 7 x 9	9 x 8 8 x 9	9 x 9	9 x 10	9 x 11	9 x 12
10 x 1	10 x 2	10 x 3	10 x 4	10 x 5	10 x 6	10 x 7	10 x 8	10 x 9	10 x 10	10 x 11	10 x 12
11 x 1	11 x 2	11 x 3	11 x 4	11 x 5	11 x 6	11 x 7	11 x 8	11 x 9	11 x 10	11 x 11	11 x 12
12 x 1	12 x 2	12 x 3	12 x 4	12 x 5	12 x 6	12 x 7	12 x 8	12 x 9	12 x 10	12 x 11	12 x 12

As you practice all of the multiplication combinations, there will be some that you "just know" and others that you are "working on" learning. To practice the combinations that are difficult for you to remember, think of a combination that you know as a clue to help you. Here are some suggestions.

$9 \times 8 = 72$ $8 \times 9 = 72$	Clue:	10 x 8 = 80	80 − 8 = 72	
$6 \times 7 = 42$ $7 \times 6 = 42$	Clue:	6 x 5 = 30	6 x 2 = 12	30 + 12 = 42
$4 \times 8 = 32$ $8 \times 4 = 32$	Clue:	2 x 8 = 16	16 + 16 = 32	

Multiplication Strategies (page 1 of 3)

In Grade 5, you are learning how to solve multiplication problems efficiently.

There are 38 rows in an auditorium, and 26 chairs in each row. How many people can sit in the auditorium?

Breaking the Numbers Apart

Georgia solved the problem 38 × 26 by breaking apart both factors.

Georgia's solution

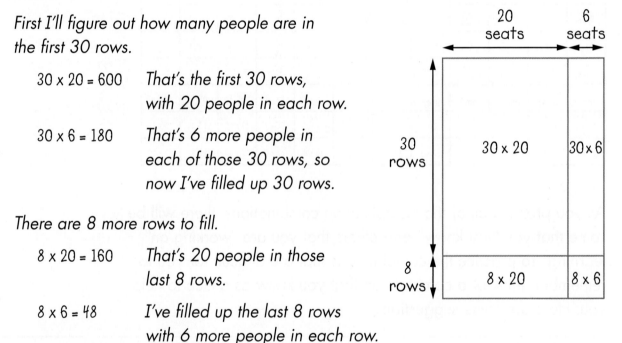

First I'll figure out how many people are in the first 30 rows.

30 x 20 = 600   *That's the first 30 rows, with 20 people in each row.*

30 x 6 = 180   *That's 6 more people in each of those 30 rows, so now I've filled up 30 rows.*

There are 8 more rows to fill.

8 x 20 = 160   *That's 20 people in those last 8 rows.*

8 x 6 = 48   *I've filled up the last 8 rows with 6 more people in each row.*

Now I add together all the parts I figured out to get the answer.

600 + 180 + 160 + 48 = **988**

988 people can sit in the auditorium.

Solve 14 × 24 by using this first step: 14 × 20 = ____?____

Multiplication Strategies (page 2 of 3)

There are 38 rows in the auditorium, and 26 chairs in each row.
How many people can sit in the auditorium?

Changing One Number to Make an Easier Problem

Benson solved the auditorium problem, 38 × 26, by
changing the 38 to 40 to make an easier problem.

Benson's solution

*I'll pretend that there are 40 rows in the
auditorium instead of 38.*

40 × 26 = 1,040   *I knew that 10 × 26 = 260.
I doubled that to get
520, and doubled that
to get 1,040.*

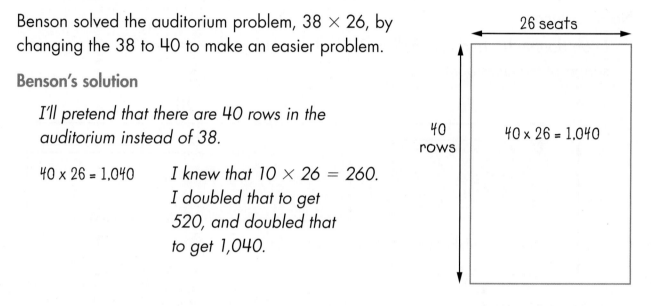

26 seats

40
rows

40 × 26 = 1,040

*So, if there were 40 rows, 1,040 people could
sit in the auditorium. But there are really only
38 rows, so I have 2 extra rows of 26 chairs.
I need to subtract those.*

2 × 26 = 52   *I need to subtract 52.
I'll do that in two parts.*

1,040 – 40 = 1,000   *First I'll subtract 40.*

1,000 – 12 = 988   *Then I'll subtract 12.*

So, **988** *people can sit in the auditorium.*

26 seats

38
rows

1,040 – 52 = 988

2 rows

Solve 19 × 14 by using this first step: 20 × 14 = ___?___

Multiplication Strategies (page 3 of 3)

A classroom measures 36 feet by 45 feet. How many 1-foot-square tiles will cover the floor?

Creating an Equivalent Problem

Nora's solution

I can double 45 and take half of 36 and pretend to change the shape of the classroom.

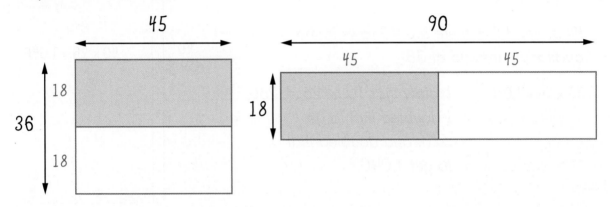

A 36-foot by 45-foot classroom needs the same amount of floor tiles as a 18-foot by 90-foot classroom.

For me, 18 × 90 is an easier problem to solve.

$$10 \times 90 = 900$$
$$8 \times 90 = 720$$
$$\overline{18 \times 90 = \textbf{1,620}}$$

1,620 tiles will cover the floor.

Solve: 35 × 22 = ___?___ × 11

Equivalent Expressions in Multiplication (page 1 of 2)

A large box holds twice as many muffins as a small box.

large box   small box

A customer ordered 7 large boxes of muffins at the bakery. The baker only had small boxes. How many small boxes of muffins should the customer buy to get the same number of muffins?

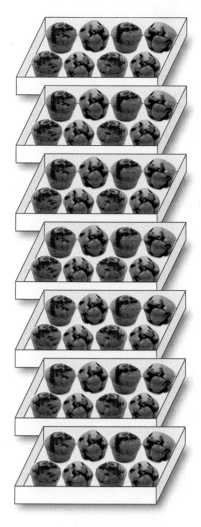

The small boxes are half the size of the large boxes. The customer should buy twice as many small boxes.

double

$$7 \times 8 = 14 \times 4$$

half

7 boxes with 8 muffins in each box

14 boxes with 4 muffins in each box

Equivalent Expressions in Multiplication (page 2 of 2)

The fifth grade is going on a field trip. The teachers planned to take 4 buses. Instead they need to take vans. How many vans do they need?

A bus holds three times as many students as a van.

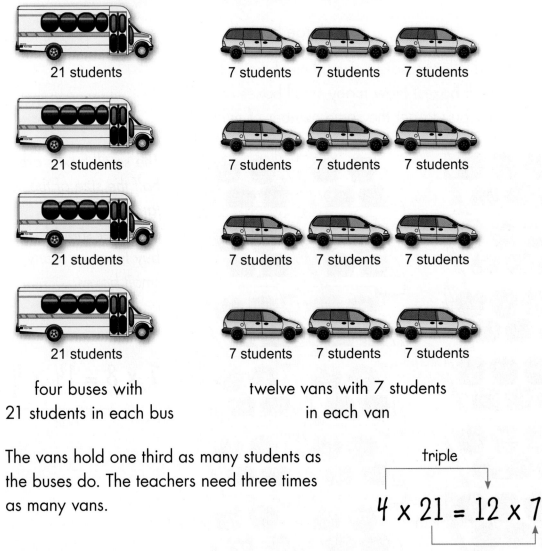

| 21 students | 7 students | 7 students | 7 students |

four buses with 21 students in each bus

twelve vans with 7 students in each van

The vans hold one third as many students as the buses do. The teachers need three times as many vans.

triple

$$4 \times 21 = 12 \times 7$$

third

Create an equivalent problem:

$4 \times 12 = \underline{\hspace{1cm}} \times \underline{\hspace{1cm}}$

Multiplication and Division Cluster Problems

Cluster problems help you use what you know about easier problems to solve harder problems.

1. Solve the problems in each cluster.

2. Use one or more of the problems in the cluster to solve the final problem, along with other problems if you need them.

Solve these cluster problems:

$24 \times 10 = \underline{240}$ $24 \times 3 = \underline{72}$

$24 \times 20 = \underline{480}$ $24 \times 30 = \underline{720}$

Now solve this problem:

$24 \times 31 = \underline{744}$

How did you solve the final problem?

I figured out that 24×30 would be 720 because $24 \times 10 = 240$, and $240 + 240 + 240 = 720$.

I need one more group of 24. That's $720 + 24 = 744$. So, $24 \times 31 = 744$.

Solve these cluster problems:

$10 \times 12 = \underline{120}$

$5 \times 12 = \underline{60}$

Now solve this problem:

$192 \div 12 = \underline{16}$

How did you solve the final problem?

I thought of $192 \div 12$ as $\underline{} \times 12 = 192$. $10 \times 12 = 120$ and $5 \times 12 = 60$, so $15 \times 12 = 120 + 60 = 180$.

I need one more 12 to get to 192. $16 \times 12 = 192$ So, $192 \div 12 = 16$.

Solve these cluster problems:

$54 \div 6 = \underline{9}$

$540 \div 6 = \underline{90}$

Now solve this problem: $6\overline{)546}$ (91)

How did you solve the final problem?

After I knew $540 \div 6 = 90$, then I knew I needed one more group of 6 because $546 = 540 + 6$. So, $546 \div 6 = 91$.

Comparing Multiplication Algorithms

Math Words
· algorithm

Some fifth graders compared these two algorithms.

An algorithm is a step-by-step procedure to solve a certain kind of problem.

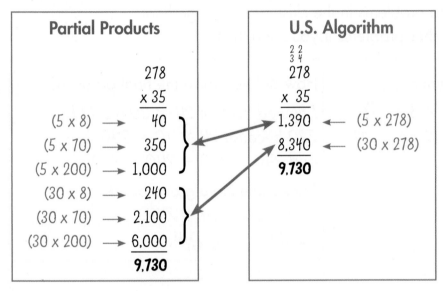

Partial Products		U.S. Algorithm

```
          Partial Products                    U.S. Algorithm
                                                  2 2
                                                  3 4
                         278                      278
                       x  35                    x  35
   (5 x 8)   →          40                     1,390  ←  (5 x 278)
   (5 x 70)  →         350                     8,340  ←  (30 x 278)
   (5 x 200) →       1,000                      9,730
   (30 x 8)  →         240
   (30 x 70) →       2,100
   (30 x 200)→       6,000
                     9,730
```

Here are some of the things the students noticed.

- *Both solutions involve breaking apart numbers.*

- *The first three numbers in the partial products algorithm are combined in the first number in the solution using the U.S. algorithm.*

- *The algorithms are mostly the same, but the U.S. algorithm notation combines steps (40 + 350 + 1,000 = 1,390).*

- *The little numbers in the U.S. algorithm stand for tens and hundreds. The 4 and the 2 above the 7 are really 40 and 20.*

Remainders: What Do You Do with the Extras?

Math Words
• remainder

When you are asked to solve division problems in context, it is important to consider the remainder to correctly answer the question asked. Here are some different story problem contexts for the division problem 186 ÷ 12.

186 people are taking a trip. One van holds 12 people. How many vans do they need?

15 vans will hold 15 × 12 or 180 people, but the other 6 people still need a ride. They need 1 more van.

Answer: **They need 16 vans.**

There are 186 pencils and 12 students. A teacher wants to give the same number of pencils to each student. How many pencils will each student get?

It does not make sense to give students half a pencil, so the teacher can keep the remaining 6 pencils.

Answer: **Each student will get 15 pencils.**

Twelve friends earned $186 by washing cars. They want to share the money equally. How much money should each person get?

Dollars can be split up into smaller amounts. Each person can get $15. The remaining $6 can be divided evenly so that every person gets another 50¢.

Answer: **Each person gets $15.50.**

Twelve people are going to share 186 crackers evenly. How many crackers does each person get?

Each person gets 15 crackers. Then the last 6 crackers can be split in half. Each person gets another half cracker.

Answer: **Each person gets $15\frac{1}{2}$ crackers.**

 **Write and solve a story problem for 153 ÷ 13.**

Division Strategies (page 1 of 2)

In Grade 5, you are learning how to solve division problems efficiently.

Here is an example of a division problem.

Janet has 1,780 marbles. She wants to put them into bags, each of which holds 32 marbles. How many full bags of marbles will she have?

Samantha solved this problem by multiplying groups of 32 to reach 1,780.

Samantha's solution

30	x	32	=	960	There are 960 marbles in 30 bags of 32.
20	x	32	=	640	There are 640 marbles in 20 bags of 32.
5	x	32	=	160	There are 160 marbles in 5 bags of 32.
55				1,760	There are 1,760 marbles in 55 bags of 32.

1,760 is as close as I can get to 1,780 with groups of 32.

Answer: 55 R20

Janet can fill 55 bags, and she will have 20 extra marbles.

Talisha solved this problem by subtracting groups of 32 from 1,780.

Talisha's solution

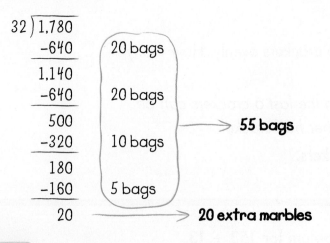

Division Strategies (page 2 of 2)

Here is another division example.

$54\overline{)2,500}$

Hana solved this problem by subtracting groups of 54 from 2,500.

Hana's solution

```
54) 2,500
  - 1,080   (20)
    1,420
  - 1,080   (20)
      340
    - 216    (4)
      124
    - 108    (2)
       16    46 R16
```

Walter solved this problem by multiplying groups of 54 to reach 2,500.

Walter's solution

```
 10    x  54  =    540

 20    x  54  =  1,080

(40)   x  54  =  2,160  →  2,160

 (4)   x  54  =    216  →    216

 (1)   x  54  =     54  →     54

 (1)   x  54  =     54  →     54
                           _____
                            2,484
```

Answer: **46 R16**

How would you solve this problem? $54\overline{)2,500}$

Fractions, Decimals, and Percents (page 1 of 2)

Math Words
• fraction • decimal • percent

Fractions, decimals, and percents are numbers that can be used to show parts of a whole.

fraction

$\frac{5}{8}$

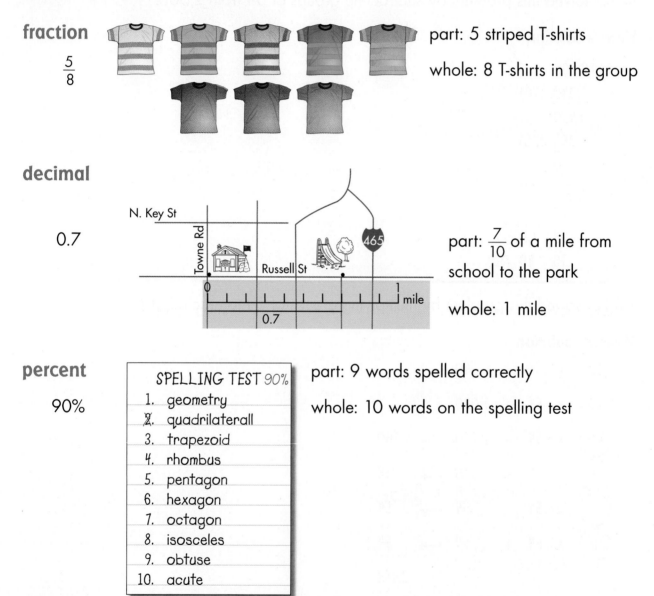

part: 5 striped T-shirts

whole: 8 T-shirts in the group

decimal

0.7

part: $\frac{7}{10}$ of a mile from school to the park

whole: 1 mile

percent

90%

SPELLING TEST 90%
1. geometry
2. quadrilaterall
3. trapezoid
4. rhombus
5. pentagon
6. hexagon
7. octagon
8. isosceles
9. obtuse
10. acute

part: 9 words spelled correctly

whole: 10 words on the spelling test

 Look in magazines and newspapers to find more everyday uses of fractions, decimals and percents.

Fractions, Decimals, and Percents (page 2 of 2)

These questions can be answered using fractions, decimals or percents.

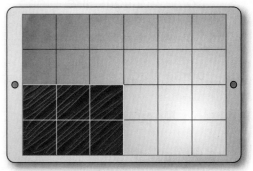

How much of the batch of brownies is left in the pan?

6 out of 24 brownies

We would most likely say:

$\frac{1}{4}$ of the brownies are in the pan.

It would also be correct to say:

25% of the brownies are in the pan.

0.25 of the brownies are in the pan.

These values are equivalent because each one represents the same quantity.

$$\frac{6}{24} = \frac{1}{4} = 25\% = 0.25$$

At the softball game, Nora went to bat 6 times and got a hit 3 of those 6 times.

Nora got a hit $\frac{1}{2}$ of the time she went to bat.

Nora got a hit 50% of the time she went to bat.

Nora's batting average for the game was .500.

These values are equivalent because each one represents the same quantity.

$$\frac{3}{6} = \frac{1}{2} = 50\% = 0.500$$

Fractions

Fractions are numbers.

Some fractions, like $\frac{1}{2}$ and $\frac{3}{4}$, are less than 1.

Some fractions, like $\frac{2}{2}$ and $\frac{4}{4}$, are equal to 1.

Some fractions, like $\frac{6}{4}$ and $\frac{3}{2}$, are greater than 1.

Fraction Notation

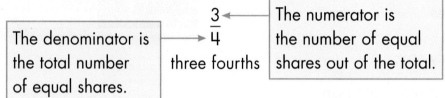

The denominator is the total number of equal shares.

$\frac{3}{4}$

three fourths

The numerator is the number of equal shares out of the total.

Charles cut a pizza into four equal pieces and ate three pieces.

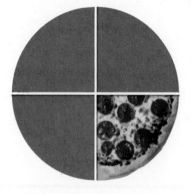

The whole pizza has four equal parts, or slices.

$\frac{3}{4}$

Charles ate three pieces.

3 out of 4 equal pieces were eaten.

Samantha has 12 marbles in her collection. Nine twelfths of her marbles are blue.

There are 12 marbles in the whole group.

$\frac{9}{12}$

Nine of the marbles are blue.

9 out of 12 equal parts are blue.

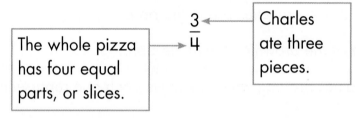

What fraction of the pizza was not eaten?

What fraction of the marbles are not blue?

Naming Fractions

In each of these examples, one whole rectangle has been divided into equal parts.

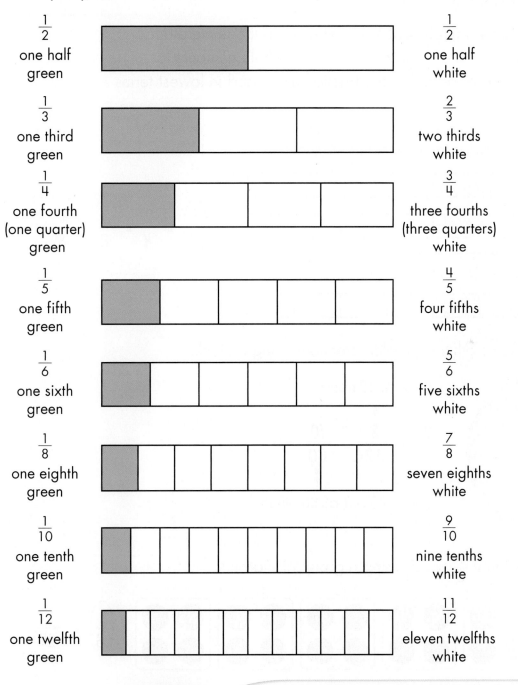

$\frac{1}{2}$
one half
green

$\frac{1}{2}$
one half
white

$\frac{1}{3}$
one third
green

$\frac{2}{3}$
two thirds
white

$\frac{1}{4}$
one fourth
(one quarter)
green

$\frac{3}{4}$
three fourths
(three quarters)
white

$\frac{1}{5}$
one fifth
green

$\frac{4}{5}$
four fifths
white

$\frac{1}{6}$
one sixth
green

$\frac{5}{6}$
five sixths
white

$\frac{1}{8}$
one eighth
green

$\frac{7}{8}$
seven eighths
white

$\frac{1}{10}$
one tenth
green

$\frac{9}{10}$
nine tenths
white

$\frac{1}{12}$
one twelfth
green

$\frac{11}{12}$
eleven twelfths
white

It's interesting that, out of all of these examples, 12 is the biggest number of parts, but that rectangle has the smallest parts.

Equivalent Fractions

Math Words

• **equivalent fractions**

Different fractions that describe the same amount are called equivalent fractions.

A fraction is expressed in lowest terms when both the numerator and the denominator are the smallest possible whole numbers for that fraction. In these examples, the fraction expressed in lowest terms is circled.

Deon used paper strips to show some equivalent fractions.

$$\left(\frac{1}{2}\right) = \frac{2}{4} = \frac{3}{6} = \frac{4}{8}$$

Janet showed some other equivalent fractions using a clock.

8 out of 12 hours

$$\left(\frac{2}{3}\right) = \frac{8}{12} = \frac{40}{60}$$

40 out of 60 minutes

Lourdes showed that $\frac{1}{6} = \frac{4}{24}$ using a group of marbles.

$$\left(\frac{1}{6}\right) = \frac{4}{24}$$

What equivalent fractions name the portion of red cubes?

Using Fractions for Quantities Greater Than One

To represent fractions greater than one, you need more than one whole.

All of these boards are the same size.

Each board is divided into 4 equal parts.

The first two whole boards are painted orange. The orange part is $\frac{8}{4}$, or 2.

On the last board, three parts are painted orange. The orange part of this board is $\frac{3}{4}$.

The total amount painted orange is $\frac{11}{4}$, or $2\frac{3}{4}$.

$$\frac{4}{4} + \frac{4}{4} + \frac{3}{4} = \frac{11}{4} = 2\frac{3}{4}$$

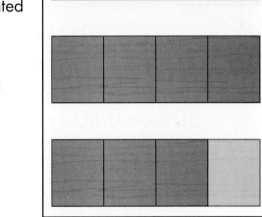

$$\frac{4}{4} = 1$$

$$\frac{4}{4} = 1$$

$$\frac{3}{4}$$

A mixed number has a whole number part and a fractional part.

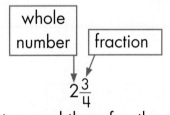

whole number | fraction

$2\frac{3}{4}$

two and three fourths

Here is another example that uses a clock as a model.

The hour hand started at 12. It made one full rotation and then moved one more hour. The total rotation is $1\frac{1}{12}$, or $\frac{13}{12}$ of the way around the clock.

? **How can you represent these fractions?** $\frac{5}{3}$ $1\frac{1}{6}$

Percents

Percent means "out of 100" or "hundredths."

Fifty percent of this 10 × 10 square is shaded.

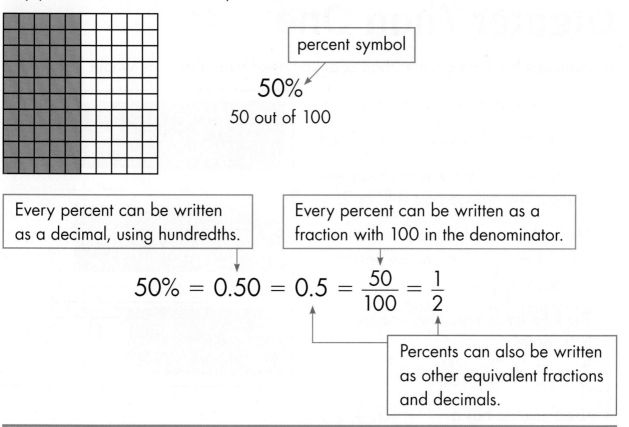

percent symbol

50%

50 out of 100

Every percent can be written as a decimal, using hundredths.

Every percent can be written as a fraction with 100 in the denominator.

$$50\% = 0.50 = 0.5 = \frac{50}{100} = \frac{1}{2}$$

Percents can also be written as other equivalent fractions and decimals.

Here are some other examples.

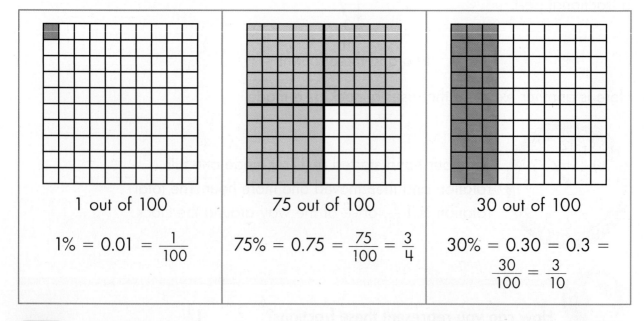

1 out of 100

$1\% = 0.01 = \frac{1}{100}$

75 out of 100

$75\% = 0.75 = \frac{75}{100} = \frac{3}{4}$

30 out of 100

$30\% = 0.30 = 0.3 = \frac{30}{100} = \frac{3}{10}$

Finding Fraction and Percent Equivalents

Two students used 10×10 grids to find percent equivalents for fractions.

Olivia worked with $\frac{3}{5}$.

Olivia's solution

$$\frac{3}{5}$$

I shaded $\frac{3}{5}$ on the 10×10 square.

Because there are five 20s in 100, every two columns on the 10×10 grid represents $\frac{1}{5}$.

I shaded 6 columns for $\frac{3}{5}$.

From looking at the 10×10 square, I know that $\frac{3}{5} = \frac{60}{100} = 60\%$.

Martin worked with $\frac{3}{8}$.

Martin's solution

$$\frac{3}{8}$$

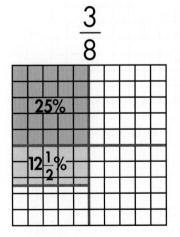

I know that $\frac{2}{8} = \frac{1}{4}$, and I know that $\frac{1}{4} = 25\%$.

So, $\frac{2}{8} = 25\%$.

$\frac{1}{8}$ is half of $\frac{2}{8}$, so $\frac{1}{8}$ is half of 25%, or $12\frac{1}{2}\%$.

$\frac{3}{8} = \frac{2}{8} + \frac{1}{8} = 25\% + 12\frac{1}{2}\% = 37\frac{1}{2}\%$

So, $\frac{3}{8} = 37\frac{1}{2}\%$.

Find the percent equivalents for these fractions:

$\frac{1}{5} = $ _____%

$\frac{5}{8} = $ _____%

Fraction and Percent Equivalents Reference

(page 1 of 2)

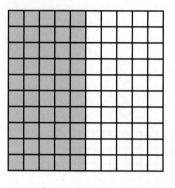

$\frac{1}{2} = 50\%$

$\frac{2}{2} = 100\%$

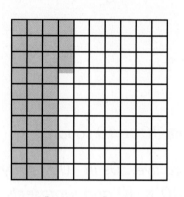

$\frac{1}{3} = 33\frac{1}{3}\%$

$\frac{2}{3} = 66\frac{2}{3}\%$

$\frac{3}{3} = 100\%$

$\frac{1}{4} = 25\%$

$\frac{2}{4} = 50\%$

$\frac{3}{4} = 75\%$

$\frac{4}{4} = 100\%$

$\frac{1}{5} = 20\%$

$\frac{2}{5} = 40\%$

$\frac{3}{5} = 60\%$

$\frac{4}{5} = 80\%$

$\frac{5}{5} = 100\%$

Fraction and Percent Equivalents Reference

(page 2 of 2)

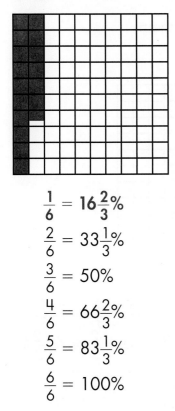

$\frac{1}{6} = 16\frac{2}{3}\%$

$\frac{2}{6} = 33\frac{1}{3}\%$

$\frac{3}{6} = 50\%$

$\frac{4}{6} = 66\frac{2}{3}\%$

$\frac{5}{6} = 83\frac{1}{3}\%$

$\frac{6}{6} = 100\%$

$\frac{1}{8} = 12\frac{1}{2}\%$

$\frac{2}{8} = 25\%$

$\frac{3}{8} = 37\frac{1}{2}\%$

$\frac{4}{8} = 50\%$

$\frac{5}{8} = 62\frac{1}{2}\%$

$\frac{6}{8} = 75\%$

$\frac{7}{8} = 87\frac{1}{2}\%$

$\frac{8}{8} = 100\%$

$\frac{1}{10} = 10\%$

$\frac{2}{10} = 20\%$

$\frac{3}{10} = 30\%$

$\frac{4}{10} = 40\%$

$\frac{5}{10} = 50\%$

$\frac{6}{10} = 60\%$

$\frac{7}{10} = 70\%$

$\frac{8}{10} = 80\%$

$\frac{9}{10} = 90\%$

$\frac{10}{10} = 100\%$

Comparing and Ordering Fractions (page 1 of 2)

Which is larger, $\frac{3}{5}$ or $\frac{2}{3}$?

Felix used the percent equivalents for these fractions to compare them.

Felix's solution

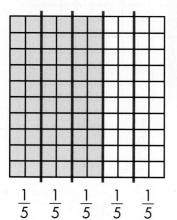

$\frac{1}{5}$ $\frac{1}{5}$ $\frac{1}{5}$ $\frac{1}{5}$ $\frac{1}{5}$

I know that $\frac{1}{5}$ = 20% because   *I know that $\frac{1}{3}$ of 100 = 30 + 3 + $\frac{1}{3}$ or $33\frac{1}{3}$.*

5 × 20 = 100. So, $\frac{3}{5}$ = 60%.   *So, $\frac{2}{3}$ of 100 is double that, 60 + 6 + $\frac{2}{3}$ or $66\frac{2}{3}$%.*

$\frac{2}{3}$ *is larger than* $\frac{3}{5}$.

$$\frac{2}{3} > \frac{3}{5}$$

Alicia and Rachel each got a pizza for lunch. Both pizzas were the same size. Alicia cut her pizza into 8 equal pieces and ate 7 pieces. Rachel cut her pizza into 6 equal pieces and ate 5 pieces. Who ate more pizza?

Stuart compared the amount of pizza left.

Stuart's solution

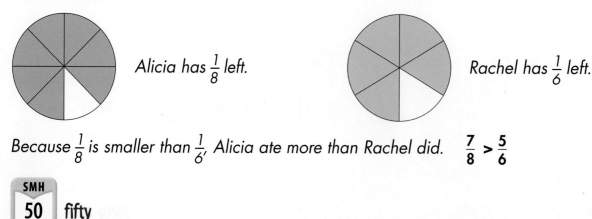

Alicia has $\frac{1}{8}$ left.   *Rachel has $\frac{1}{6}$ left.*

Because $\frac{1}{8}$ is smaller than $\frac{1}{6}$, Alicia ate more than Rachel did. $\frac{7}{8} > \frac{5}{6}$

Comparing and Ordering Fractions (page 2 of 2)

What is the order of these fractions from least to greatest?

$$\frac{7}{8}, \frac{7}{12}, \frac{4}{10}$$

Hana used what she knew about $\frac{1}{2}$ and 1 to put the fractions in order.

Hana's solution

$\frac{7}{8}$ is the largest. It is close to 1.

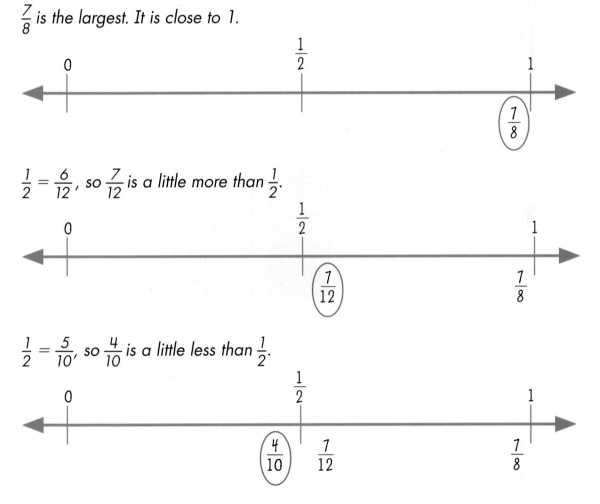

$\frac{1}{2} = \frac{6}{12}$, so $\frac{7}{12}$ is a little more than $\frac{1}{2}$.

$\frac{1}{2} = \frac{5}{10}$, so $\frac{4}{10}$ is a little less than $\frac{1}{2}$.

So, from least to greatest, the fractions are $\frac{4}{10}, \frac{7}{12}, \frac{7}{8}$.

Which is larger, $\frac{3}{4}$ or $\frac{4}{5}$?

Adding Fractions (page 1 of 2)

$$\frac{1}{2} + \frac{3}{5} =$$

Samantha used shaded strips to solve this problem.

Samantha's solution

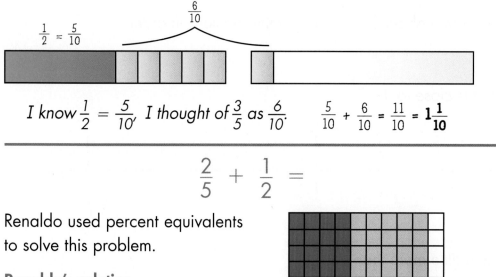

$$\frac{1}{2} = \frac{5}{10}$$

$$\frac{6}{10}$$

I know $\frac{1}{2} = \frac{5}{10}$, I thought of $\frac{3}{5}$ as $\frac{6}{10}$. $\quad$ $\frac{5}{10} + \frac{6}{10} = \frac{11}{10} = 1\frac{1}{10}$

$$\frac{2}{5} + \frac{1}{2} =$$

Renaldo used percent equivalents to solve this problem.

Renaldo's solution

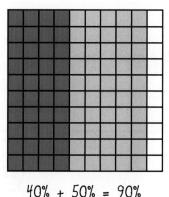

$\frac{2}{5}$ is the same as $\frac{4}{10}$, or 40%.

$\frac{1}{2}$ is 50 out of 100, or 50%.

$$40\% + 50\% = 90\%$$
$$\frac{2}{5} + \frac{1}{2} = \frac{9}{10}$$

$$\frac{1}{2} + \frac{1}{6} =$$

Tamira used a number line to solve this problem.

Tamira's solution

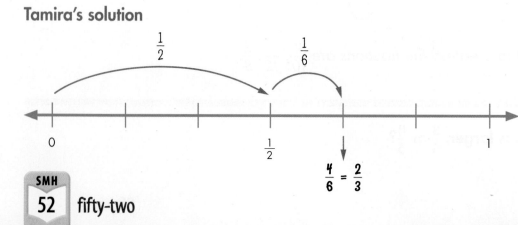

$$\frac{1}{2}$$ $$\frac{1}{6}$$

0 $\qquad$ $\frac{1}{2}$ $\qquad$ 1

$$\frac{4}{6} = \frac{2}{3}$$

Adding Fractions (page 2 of 2)

$$\frac{3}{4} + \frac{1}{6} =$$

Deon used a clock model to solve this problem.

Deon's solution

Starting at 12:00 and moving $\frac{3}{4}$ of the way around, you land at 9:00.

Moving $\frac{1}{6}$ is 2 hours more, or 11:00.

That is the same as $\frac{11}{12}$ of the way around the clock.

So, $\frac{3}{4} + \frac{1}{6} = \frac{11}{12}$.

$$\frac{3}{4} + \frac{5}{8} + \frac{1}{2} =$$

Yumiko used shaded strips to solve this problem.

Yumiko's solution

Both $\frac{3}{4}$ and $\frac{5}{8}$ are greater than $\frac{1}{2}$, so the answer will be more than 1 whole.

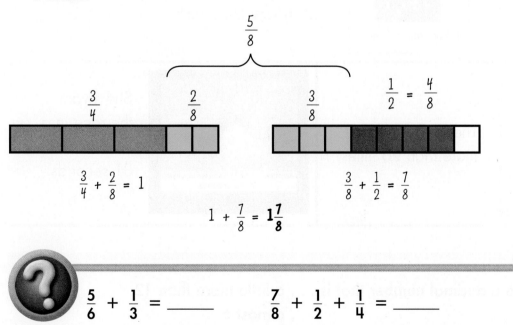

$$\frac{3}{4} + \frac{2}{8} = 1$$

$$\frac{3}{8} + \frac{1}{2} = \frac{7}{8}$$

$$1 + \frac{7}{8} = 1\frac{7}{8}$$

$$\frac{5}{6} + \frac{1}{3} = \underline{\qquad}$$ $$\frac{7}{8} + \frac{1}{2} + \frac{1}{4} = \underline{\qquad}$$

Decimals

Math Words
• decimal

The system we use to write numbers is called the decimal number system. *Decimal* means that the number is based on tens.

Some numbers, like 2.5 and 0.3, include a decimal point. The digits to the right of the decimal point are part of the number that is less than 1.

Here are some examples you may know of decimal numbers that are less than one.

$0.5 = \frac{5}{10} = \frac{1}{2}$	$0.25 = \frac{25}{100} = \frac{1}{4}$

Numbers such as 0.5 and 0.25 are sometimes called decimal fractions.

Some decimal numbers have a whole number part and a part that is less than 1, just as mixed numbers do.

$1.5 = 1\frac{5}{10} = 1\frac{1}{2}$	$12.75 = 12\frac{75}{100} = 12\frac{3}{4}$

Here are some examples of the ways we use decimals everyday:

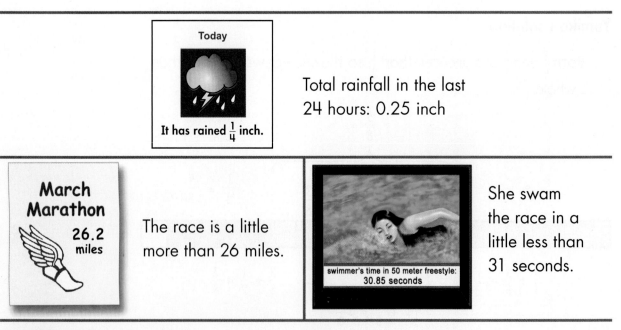

Today

It has rained $\frac{1}{4}$ inch.

Total rainfall in the last 24 hours: 0.25 inch

March Marathon
26.2 miles

The race is a little more than 26 miles.

swimmer's time in 50 meter freestyle: 30.85 seconds

She swam the race in a little less than 31 seconds.

? **Write a decimal number that is . . . a little more than 12.**
. . . almost 6.
. . . more than $\frac{3}{4}$ and less than 1.

Representing Decimals

(page 1 of 2)

Math Words
• tenths
• hundredths

In each of the following examples, the whole square has been divided into equal parts and the amount shaded is named.

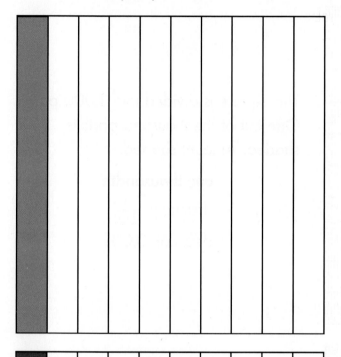

This square is divided into 10 parts. One out of the ten parts is shaded. Amount shaded:

one tenth

fraction: $\frac{1}{10}$

decimal: 0.1

This square is divided into 100 parts. One out of the hundred parts is shaded. Amount shaded:

one hundredth

fraction: $\frac{1}{100}$

decimal: 0.01

Representing Decimals

(page 2 of 2)

In each of the following examples, the whole square has been divided into equal parts and the amount shaded is named.

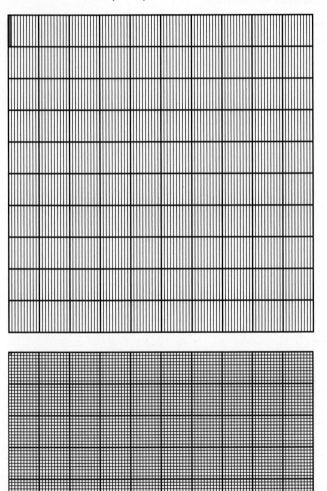

This square is divided into 1,000 parts. One out of the thousand parts is shaded. Amount shaded:

one thousandth

fraction: $\frac{1}{1000}$

decimal: 0.001

This square is divided into 10,000 parts. One out of the ten thousand parts is shaded. Amount shaded:

one ten-thousandth

fraction: $\frac{1}{10000}$

decimal: 0.0001

Can you prove that the thousandths square is divided into one thousand parts without counting them?

Place Value of Decimals

As with whole numbers, the value of a digit changes depending on its place in a decimal number.

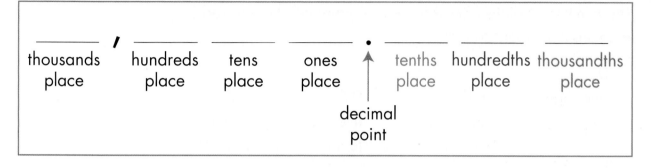

thousands place | hundreds place | tens place | ones place | tenths place | hundredths place | thousandths place

decimal point

In these three examples the digit 5 has different **values:**

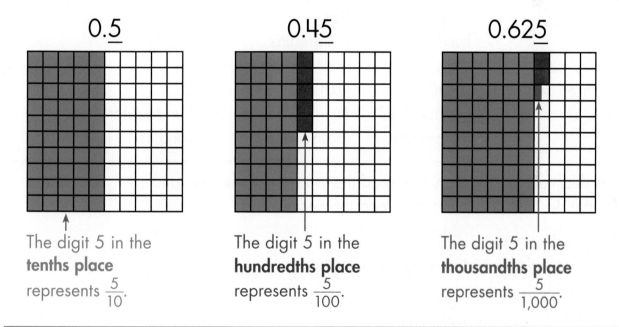

0.<u>5</u>

0.4<u>5</u>

0.62<u>5</u>

The digit 5 in the **tenths place** represents $\frac{5}{10}$.

The digit 5 in the **hundredths place** represents $\frac{5}{100}$.

The digit 5 in the **thousandths place** represents $\frac{5}{1,000}$.

Look at the values of the digits in this number:

1.375 (one and three hundred seventy-five thousandths or $1\frac{375}{1,000}$)

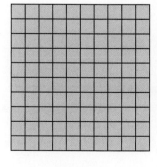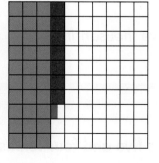

1   the digit 1 represents one whole
0.3   the digit 3 represents three tenths
0.07   the digit 7 represents seven hundredths
0.005   the digit 5 represents five thousandths

1.375 = 1 + 0.3 + 0.07 + 0.005

Reading and Writing Decimals

The number of digits after the decimal point tells how to read a decimal number.

0 . __
one digit

0.4	0.5	0.7
four	five	seven
tenths	tenths	tenths

0 . __ __
two digits

0.40	0.05	0.35
forty	five	thirty-five
hundredths	hundredths	hundredths

0 . __ __ __
three digits

0.400	0.005	0.250
four hundred	five	two hundred fifty
thousandths	thousandths	thousandths

For decimals greater than one, read the whole number, say "and" for the decimal point, and then read the decimal.

3 . 75
three and seventy-five hundredths

10 . 5
ten and five tenths

200 . 05
two hundred and five hundredths

17 . 345
seventeen and three hundred forty-five thousandths

Say this number: 40.35

Write this number: three hundred five and four tenths

Equivalent Decimals, Fractions, and Percents

(page 1 of 2)

You can describe the shaded part of this 10 × 10 square in different ways.

How many tenths are shaded?

0.5   (5 out of 10 columns are shaded)

How many hundredths are shaded?

0.50   (50 out of 100 squares are shaded)

> These decimals are equal:
> 0.5 = 0.50

There are many ways to represent the same part of a whole with decimals, fractions, and percents.

$$0.5 = 0.50 = \frac{1}{2} = \frac{5}{10} = \frac{50}{100} = 50\%$$

Now look at this 10 × 10 square.

How many tenths are shaded?

0.2   (2 out of 10 columns are shaded)

How many hundredths are shaded?

0.20   (20 out of 100 squares are shaded)

$$0.2 = 0.20 = \frac{2}{10} = \frac{1}{5} = \frac{20}{100} = 20\%$$

How many tenths are shaded?
How many hundredths are shaded?
What fractional parts are shaded?
What percent is shaded?

Equivalent Decimals, Fractions, and Percents

(page 2 of 2)

Find the decimal equivalents for $\frac{1}{8}$, $\frac{4}{8}$, and $\frac{5}{8}$.

Several students used different strategies to find the solution to this problem.

Tavon's solution

I used my calculator to figure out $\frac{1}{8}$. The fraction $\frac{1}{8}$ is the same as $1 \div 8$, and the answer is 0.125.

$$\frac{1}{8} = 0.125$$

Margaret's solution

I got the same answer a different way.
$\frac{1}{8}$ is half of $\frac{1}{4}$ and $\frac{1}{4} = 25\%$. So, $\frac{1}{8}$ is half of 25%. That's $12\frac{1}{2}\%$, or 0.125.

$$\frac{1}{8} = 0.125$$

Avery's solution

To solve $\frac{4}{8}$, I just thought about equivalent fractions. $\frac{4}{8}$ is really easy because it is the same as $\frac{1}{2}$.

$$\frac{4}{8} = \frac{1}{2} = 0.5$$

Samantha's solution

I imagined $\frac{5}{8}$ shaded on a 10 × 10 square. That fills up $\frac{1}{2}$ plus one more eighth.

$$\frac{5}{8} = \frac{1}{2} + \frac{1}{8}$$
$$= 50\% + 12\frac{1}{2}\%$$
$$= 62\frac{1}{2}\%$$
$$\frac{5}{8} = 0.625$$

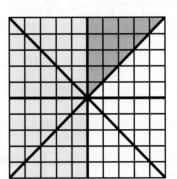

Find the decimal equivalents for these fractions:

$$\frac{6}{8} \qquad \frac{7}{8} \qquad \frac{8}{8}$$

Comparing and Ordering Decimals (page 1 of 2)

Which is larger, 0.35 or 0.6?

Rachel's solution

Rachel used 10 × 10 squares to compare the decimals.

I thought 0.35 was bigger because it has more numbers in it. But when I drew the picture, I saw that 0.6 is the same as $\frac{60}{100}$, which is more than $\frac{35}{100}$.

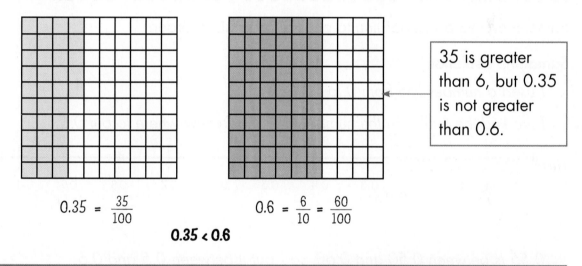

$0.35 = \frac{35}{100}$

$0.6 = \frac{6}{10} = \frac{60}{100}$

35 is greater than 6, but 0.35 is not greater than 0.6.

0.35 < 0.6

Three students ran a 400-meter race.

Place their times in order from fastest to slowest.

Walter looked at place value to put the times in order.

NAME	TIME (SECONDS)
CHARLES	51.12
MARTIN	50.90
STUART	51.04

The least number of seconds is the fastest time.

Walter's solution

First Place:	Martin, 50.90 seconds	*I looked at the whole number parts. Since 50 < 51, 50.90 is the fastest time.*
Second Place:	Stuart, 51.04 seconds	*Stuart and Charles each finished in a little more than 51 seconds.*
Third Place:	Charles, 51.12 seconds	*4 hundredths is less than 12 hundredths, so Stuart was faster than Charles.*

Comparing and Ordering Decimals (page 2 of 2)

What is the order of these decimals from least to greatest?

0.8	0.55	0.625
eight tenths	fifty-five hundredths	six hundred twenty-five thousandths

Samantha used a number line to put the decimals in order.

Samantha's solution

I used a number line from 0 to 1.

I marked the tenths on the number line and I knew where to put 0.8.

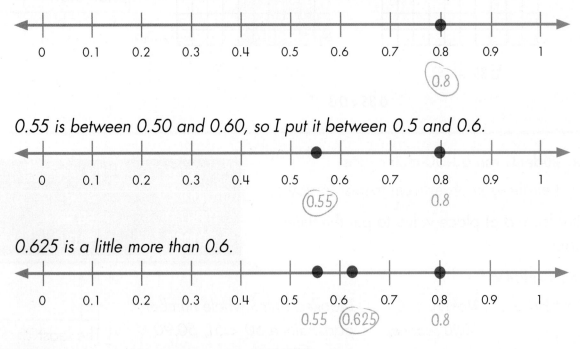

0.55 is between 0.50 and 0.60, so I put it between 0.5 and 0.6.

0.625 is a little more than 0.6.

0.55 < 0.625 < 0.8

Which is larger, 0.65 or 0.4?
Which is larger, 0.4 or 0.375?

Adding Decimals (page 1 of 3)

Deon, Alicia, and Zachary used different strategies to add these decimals.

$$0.4 + 0.25 =$$

Deon's solution

I used different colors to shade the decimals on a 10 × 10 square.

*The total is 6 tenths and 5 hundredths, or **0.65**.*

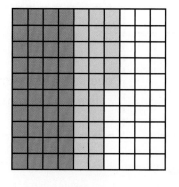

Alicia's solution

$$\begin{array}{r} 0.40 \\ + 0.25 \\ \hline \mathbf{0.65} \end{array}$$

0.4 is the same as 0.40.

0.4 is close to $\frac{1}{2}$ and 0.25 is the same as $\frac{1}{4}$, so I knew the answer should be close to $\frac{3}{4}$, or 0.75.

Zachary's solution

So, I added by place. I added the tenths, and then the hundredths.

0.4 is 4 tenths and 0 hundredths.

0.25 is 2 tenths and 5 hundredths.

0.4 + 0.2 = 0.6

*6 tenths and 5 hundredths is **0.65**.*

Since 25 + 4 = 29, at first I thought the answer would be 0.29, but I could tell from Deon's picture that 0.29 didn't make sense.

Adding Decimals (page 2 of 3)

Shandra, Joshua, Nora, and Lourdes solved this addition problem in different ways.

What is the sum of these decimals?

0.6 six tenths	0.125 one hundred twenty-five thousandths	0.45 forty-five hundredths

Shandra's solution

I broke up the numbers and added by place.

First I added all of the tenths.
Next I added the hundredths.
Then I added everything together.

$0.6 + 0.1 + 0.4 = 1.1$

$0.02 + 0.05 = 0.07$

$1.1 + 0.07 + 0.005 = \textbf{1.175}$

> I knew that the answer would be more than 1 because in the tenths I saw 0.6 and 0.4, which add up to 1.

Joshua's solution

I used equivalents. I just thought of all the numbers as thousandths; then I added them.

$0.6 = 0.600$

$0.45 = 0.450$

$600 + 450 = 1,050$

$1,050 + 125 = 1,175$

Since 1,000 thousandths is 1, the answer is **1.175**.

Adding Decimals (page 3 of 3)

$$0.6 + 0.125 + 0.45 = \underline{\ ?\ }$$

Walter's solution

I did it kind of like Joshua, but I lined up the numbers and then added.

```
  0.600
  0.125
+ 0.450
  1.100
  0.070
+ 0.005
  1.175
```

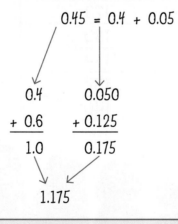

You can't just add like this because the decimal place values have to match.

```
    6
  125
+  45
```

Lourdes' solution

I split up 0.45 into 4 tenths and 5 hundredths.

$$0.45 = 0.4 + 0.05$$

```
  0.4          0.050
+ 0.6        + 0.125
  1.0          0.175
```

```
        1.175
```

You may notice that you are using the same strategies to add decimals that you used to add whole numbers. You can review those addition strategies on pages 8–9 in this handbook.

0.65 + 0.3 = _____   **0.375 + 0.2 = _____**

Tables and Graphs (page 1 of 2)

This table and the graph on page 67 show how Olivia grew between the ages of 2 and 10 based on this growth story.

Olivia was 86 centimeters tall on her second birthday. Between the ages of 2 and 6 she grew quickly, about 10 centimeters per year. Then she grew at a slower rate. She was 140 centimeters tall when she was 10 years old.

This column shows Olivia's age.

This column shows Olivia's height.

Olivia's Growth

Age (years)	Height (centimeters)
2	86
3	95
4	105
5	113
6	123
7	130
8	134
9	137
10	140

This row shows that Olivia was 105 centimeters tall when she was 4 years old.

Tables and Graphs (page 2 of 2)

This graph shows the information about Olivia's growth given in the table on page 66.

Math Words
- **vertical axis**
- **y-axis**
- **horizontal axis**
- **x-axis**

The vertical axis, or *y*-axis, shows height.

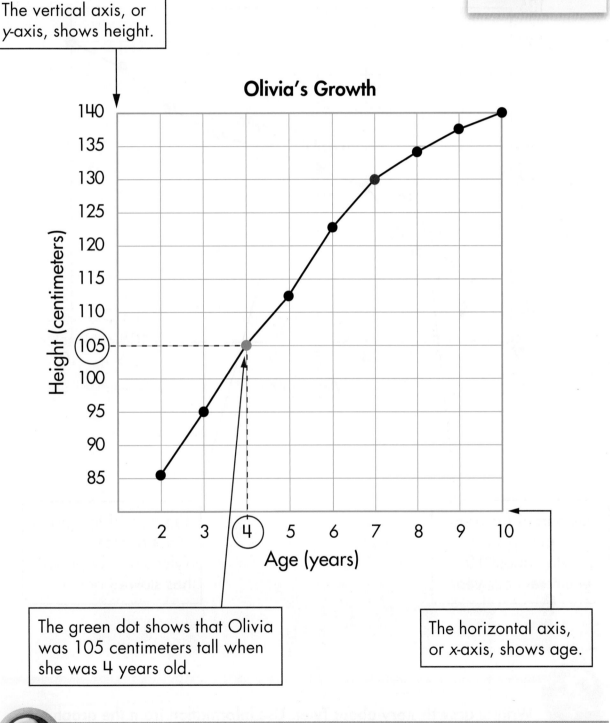

Olivia's Growth

The green dot shows that Olivia was 105 centimeters tall when she was 4 years old.

The horizontal axis, or *x*-axis, shows age.

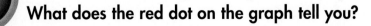

What does the red dot on the graph tell you?

Faster and Slower Growth

This graph shows how Tyler grew between the ages of 2 and 10.

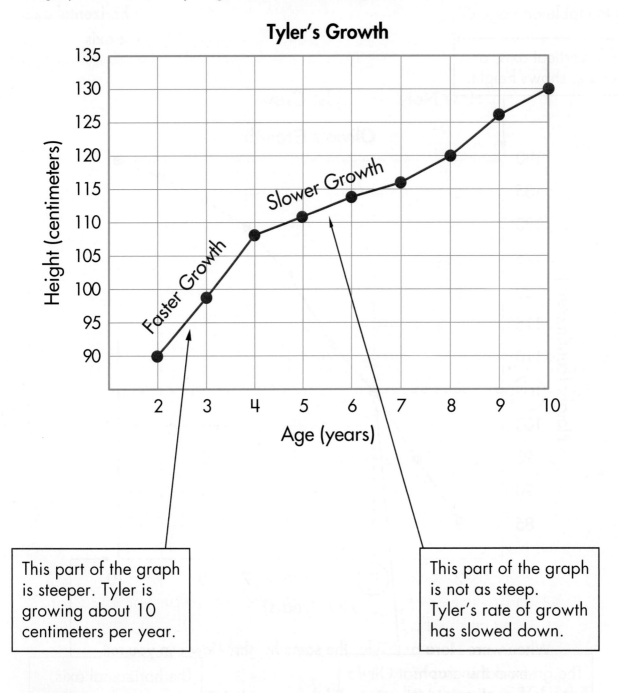

Tyler's Growth

Faster Growth

Slower Growth

This part of the graph is steeper. Tyler is growing about 10 centimeters per year.

This part of the graph is not as steep. Tyler's rate of growth has slowed down.

? Write a growth story about Tyler. Use information from the graph to describe how he grew from age 2 to age 10.

Telling Stories from Line Graphs

This graph shows how Nora and Tyler grew between the ages of 2 and 10.

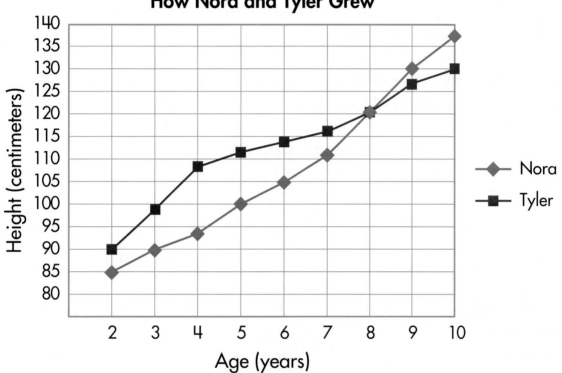

How Nora and Tyler Grew

◆ Nora
■ Tyler

Use the graph to answer these questions.

Who was taller at age 2? How much taller? Who was taller at age 10? How much taller?

When were Nora and Tyler the same height? How can you tell from the graph?

Answer these riddles. How did the graph help?

> *I grew quickly until I was 7 years old and even more quickly between the ages of 7 and 10. Who am I?*

> *I grew quickly from ages 2 to 4. Then I grew more slowly until the age of 7, when I grew more quickly again. Who am I?*

Growing at a Constant Rate (page 1 of 2)

In some situations, change happens at a constant rate.

On the planet Rhomaar, every animal grows according to a particular pattern. The Whippersnap is an animal that lives on the planet Rhomaar and grows at a constant rate.

This table shows how the Whippersnap grows. At birth, the Whippersnap is 20 centimeters tall. It grows 5 centimeters each year.

Whippersnap's Growth

Age (years)	Height (centimeters)
0 (birth)	20
1	25
2	30
3	35
4	40
5	45
6	50
7	55
8	60
9	65
10	70
15	95
20	?

+5 centimeters each year

This row shows that the Whippersnap is 40 centimeters tall at age 4.

Beginning here, the table skips some rows.

How tall is the Whippersnap when it is 20 years old? How did you figure that out?

Growing at a Constant Rate (page 2 of 2)

This graph shows the information about the Whippersnap's growth given in the table on page 70.

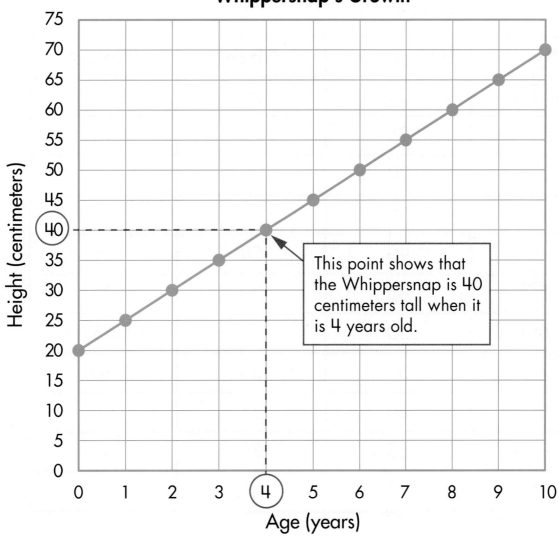

Whippersnap's Growth

This point shows that the Whippersnap is 40 centimeters tall when it is 4 years old.

Why do you think the points on the graph form a straight line?

Comparing Rates of Growth

(page 1 of 2)

The Whippersnap, the Frizzle, and the Bluespot all live on the planet Rhomaar.

Each grows at a constant rate.

The table shows how they grow from birth to age 10.

Age	Whippersnap	Frizzle	Bluespot
0 (birth)	20	20	5
1	25	22	10
2	30	24	15
3	35	26	20
4	40	28	25
5	45	30	30
6	50	32	35
7	55	34	40
8	60	36	45
9	65	38	50
10	70	40	55

Comparing Rates of Growth

(page 2 of 2)

This graph shows how they grow from birth to age 10.

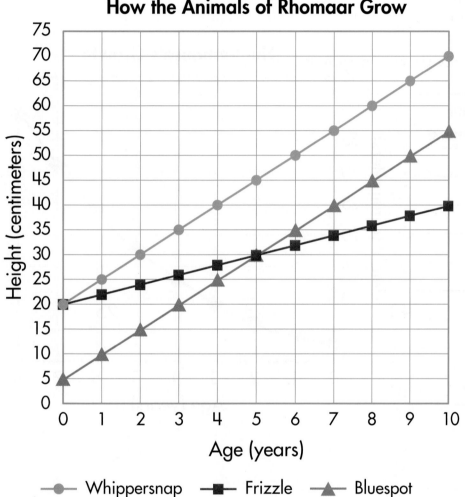

How the Animals of Rhomaar Grow

Height (centimeters) vs. Age (years)

—•— Whippersnap —■— Frizzle —▲— Bluespot

Are the Bluespot and the Frizzle ever the same height at the same time?
How does the graph show that?
How does the table show that?
Will the Bluespot and the Whippersnap ever be the same height
at the same time?
How does the graph show that?
How does the table show that?

Growing at a Changing Rate

The Huntermouse is another animal that lives on the planet Rhomaar.
Like the other animals on the planet Rhomaar, the Huntermouse
grows according to a particular pattern. However, it does *not*
grow at a constant rate.

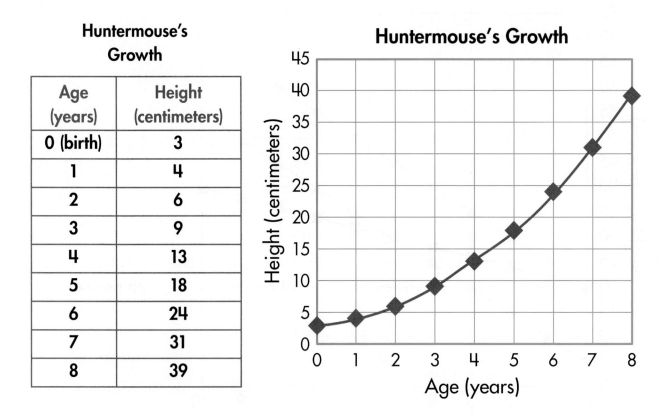

Huntermouse's Growth

Age (years)	Height (centimeters)
0 (birth)	3
1	4
2	6
3	9
4	13
5	18
6	24
7	31
8	39

Huntermouse's Growth

Compare the Huntermouse's growth pattern to the growth patterns
of the other animals of Rhomaar described on pages 70–73.
What is different about the Huntermouse's growth pattern?
What do you notice about the table? What do you notice about the graph?
Can you figure out how tall the Huntermouse will be when it is 10 years old?
Why or why not?

The Penny Jar (page 1 of 2)

In some Penny Jars, the total number of pennies increases at a constant rate.

The rule for the Penny Jar shown below is:

Start with 3 pennies and add 5 pennies each round.

Start	Round 1	Round 2	Round 5
Total: 3 pennies	Total: 8 pennies	Total: 13 pennies	Total: 28 pennies

How many pennies will be in the jar after the 4th round?

Jill drew this picture to find out.

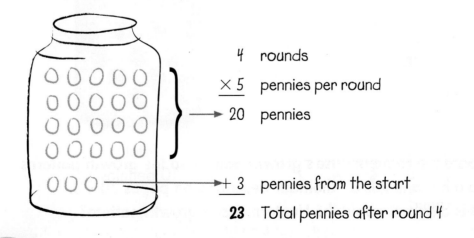

4	rounds
× 5	pennies per round
20	pennies
+ 3	pennies from the start
23	Total pennies after round 4

How many pennies will be in the jar after the 7th round?
How many pennies will be in the jar after the 10th round?

The Penny Jar (page 2 of 2)

In another Penny Jar, the total number of pennies does not increase at a constant rate.

Number of Rounds	Total Number of Pennies
Start	1
1	3
2	6
3	10
4	15
5	21
6	28
7	36

In this Penny Jar situation, the number of pennies added increases by 1 each time, like this:

Round 1: 2 pennies added

Round 2: 3 pennies added

Round 3: 4 pennies added

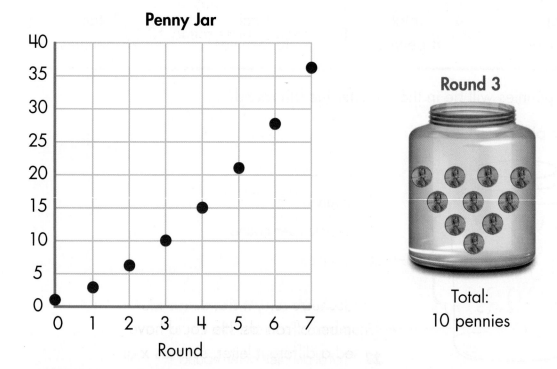

Penny Jar

Round 3

Total: 10 pennies

If this pattern continues, how many pennies will be in the jar after round 10? Why do you think the points on this graph do not form a straight line?

Writing Rules to Describe Change (page 1 of 2)

The rule for the Penny Jar below is:

Start with 8 pennies and add 5 pennies each round.

How many pennies will there be in the jar after 10 rounds?

10	rounds
× 5	pennies per round
50	pennies
+ 8	pennies from the start
58	Total pennies after round 10

These students wrote a rule for the number of pennies for any round using words or an arithmetic expression.

Terrence's rule: You multiply the number of rounds by 5.
Then you add 8 because that is the number
of pennies in the jar at the beginning.

Janet's rule: Round x 5 + 8

Joshua's rule: $8 + (5 \times n)$ ←

In Joshua's rule, n stands for the number of rounds. He could have used a different letter, such as x or r.

Use one of these rules or your own rule to find out how many pennies will be in the jar after round 30.

Writing Rules to Describe Change (page 2 of 2)

Here is a series of rectangles made out of square tiles.
The sides of each square tile are 1 centimeter.

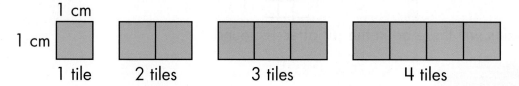

1 cm
1 cm
1 tile   2 tiles   3 tiles   4 tiles

Some students looked at how the perimeter changed as the rectangle grew.

Number of Square Tiles	Perimeter of Rectangle
1	4
2	6
3	8
4	10
5	12

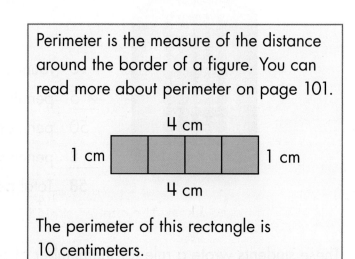

Perimeter is the measure of the distance around the border of a figure. You can read more about perimeter on page 101.

4 cm
1 cm   1 cm
4 cm

The perimeter of this rectangle is 10 centimeters.

Some students discussed the rules they wrote for determining the perimeter for any rectangle in this pattern using any number of square tiles.

Stuart: *You double the number of squares and add 2.
My rule is P = 2n + 2.*

Tamira: *I see it differently. You add 1 to the number of squares
and then you double that. My rule is P = (1 + n) × 2.*

Samantha: *My way is almost the same as Stuart's. I add the number
of squares to itself, and then add 1 and 1 for the ends.
My rule is P = n + n + 1 + 1.*

**Use one of these rules or your own rule to determine
the perimeter of a rectangle in this pattern made of 50 tiles.**

Working with Data

Math Words
• **data**

Data are pieces of information. You can collect data by counting something, measuring something, or doing experiments.

People collect data to gather information they want to know about the world.

By collecting, representing, and analyzing data, you can answer questions like these:

How long can you stand on one foot?

How safe is our playground?

Which bridge design will hold the most weight?

Which group watches more television per day, fifth graders or adults?

Working with data is a process.

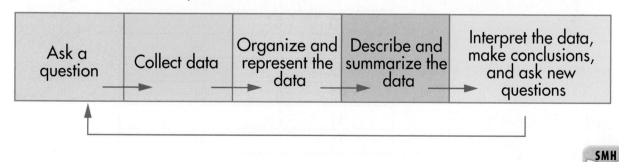

| Ask a question | Collect data | Organize and represent the data | Describe and summarize the data | Interpret the data, make conclusions, and ask new questions |

Designing an Experiment and Collecting Data

Felix and Janet wondered:

> What kind of paper bridge will hold the most weight?

They designed an experiment to find out. They built different kinds of bridges out of paper and tested the strength of the bridges by counting how many pennies the bridges would hold before collapsing.

Janet designed an accordion bridge.

Felix and Janet carried out 15 trials of their experiment using the accordion bridge. Each time, they recorded the number of pennies the accordion bridge could hold.

Accordion Bridge Experiment	
Trial	Number of Pennies
1	30
2	38
3	38
4	15
5	27
6	43
7	24
8	44
9	24
10	72
11	38
12	46
13	21
14	30
15	31

Organizing and Representing Data

Felix and Janet chose different ways to represent the accordion bridge data given on page 80.

Janet represented the data in a line plot.

Each X on the line plot stands for one trial.

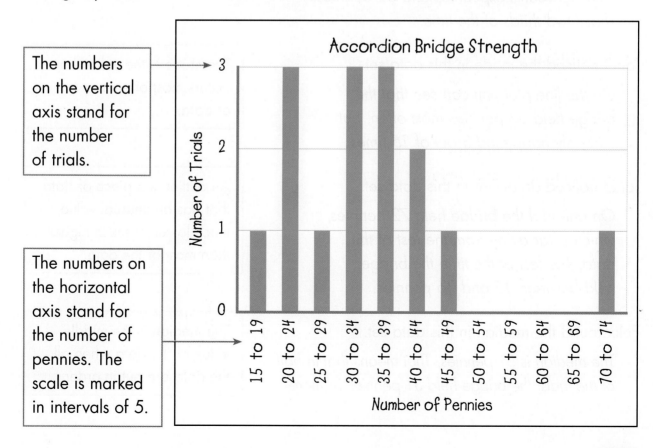

Felix used his knowledge of bar graphs to represent the data. He did not want to have lots of little bars. He thought it would be easier to see the data if he grouped the numbers into intervals, like 15–19, 20–24, and so forth.

The numbers on the vertical axis stand for the number of trials.

The numbers on the horizontal axis stand for the number of pennies. The scale is marked in intervals of 5.

Describing and Summarizing Data

Here are some of the observations that Janet and Felix made about their accordion bridge data, given on pages 80 and 81.

Janet noticed the range of this data set.

The data ranged from 15 pennies to 72 pennies. The accordion bridge always held at least 15 pennies. The most pennies it could hold was 72, but that only happened once.

The range is the difference between the highest value and the lowest value in a set of data.

In these data, the range is 57 pennies:

$$72 - 15 = 57$$
highest value   lowest value   range

Felix found an interval where most of the data are concentrated.

Ten out of fifteen times, the accordion bridge held between 20 pennies and 39 pennies. That's two thirds of the time.

Janet noticed the mode in this data set.

On the line plot you can see that the bridge held 38 pennies most often, but that only happened 3 out of 15 times.

The mode is the value that occurs most often in a set of data.

Janet noticed an outlier in this data set.

On one trial the bridge held 72 pennies, which is far away from the rest of the data. The rest of the time the bridge held between 15 and 46 pennies.

An outlier is a piece of data that has an unusual value, much lower or much higher than most of the data.

Felix found the median in this data set.

The median is 31 pennies. That means that in half of the trials, the bridge held 31 pennies or more.

The median is the middle value of the data when all the data are put in order.

Finding the Median

(page 1 of 2)

The median is the middle value of the data when all of the data values are put in order.

How long can adults balance on their left feet?

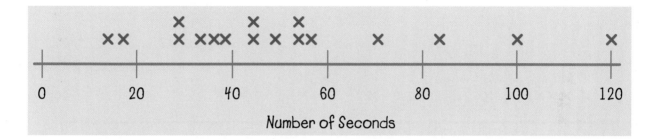

Number of Seconds

Here are the 17 values listed in order:

15, 17, 29, 29, 31, 35, 38, 45, 45, 49, 53, 53, 55, 70, 82, 100, 120

↑
median

Half of the adults balanced on their left feet for 45 seconds or less, and half of them balanced for 45 seconds or more.

> The middle value is 45, so the median value is 45 seconds.

Finding the Median

(page 2 of 2)

When a set of data has an even number of values, the median is between the two middle values.

How long can students balance on their left feet?

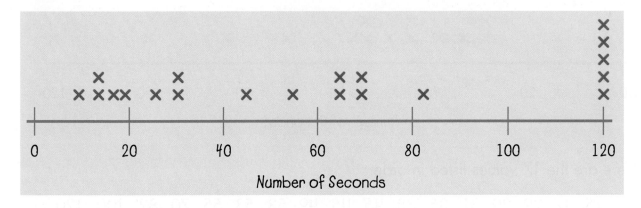

Number of Seconds

Here are the 20 values listed in order:

10, 14, 14, 18, 19, 25, 30, 30, 45, 55, 65, 65, 70, 70, 82, 120, 120, 120, 120, 120

↑
median

There are as many students in the group who balanced on their left feet for 60 seconds or less as there are students who balanced for 60 seconds or more.

> Since the middle values are not the same, the median is midway between the two values 55 and 65. The median is 60 seconds.

How would you compare these adults and students? Which group has the better balancers, or are they about the same?

Comparing Two Sets of Data (page 1 of 4)

Math Words
• double bar graph

Janet and Felix continued the bridge strength experiment discussed on pages 80 and 81. They tested a different type of bridge.

Felix designed a folded beam bridge.

Felix and Janet carried out 15 trials of their experiment. Each time, they recorded the number of pennies the beam bridge could hold.

Beam Bridge Experiment	
Trial	Number of Pennies
1	15
2	24
3	37
4	29
5	68
6	64
7	55
8	47
9	47
10	74
11	35
12	38
13	57
14	50
15	32

Comparing Two Sets of Data (page 2 of 4)

Janet and Felix created representations so they could easily compare the data from the accordion bridge (page 80) to the data from the beam bridge (page 85).

Janet represented each set of data on a line plot. She used the same scale from 0 pennies to 80 pennies on both line plots to make it easier to compare them.

Janet's representation

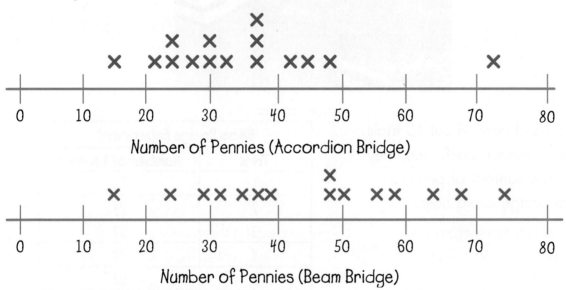

Here is what Janet noticed:

- *The range of the data for both bridges is almost the same: from 15 to 72 for the accordion bridge and from 15 to 74 for the beam bridge.*

- *Almost all of the accordion bridge data are clustered in the lower part of the graph, from 15 to 49 pennies. It is easy to see that there is only one high value for the accordion bridge.*

- *The number of pennies held by the accordion bridge is mostly in the 20s, 30s, and 40s. The beam bridge data are more spread out. They go as low as the accordion bridge, but they keep going higher, into the 50s and 60s.*

Comparing Two Sets of Data (page 3 of 4)

> This key shows that the red bars represent the accordion bridge trials and the blue bars represent the beam bridge trials.

Felix represented the data on a double bar graph.

Felix's representation

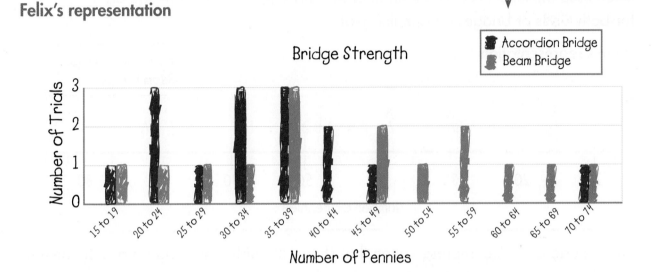

Bridge Strength

Accordion Bridge
Beam Bridge

Based on what they noticed in the data they compared, Janet and Felix came to these conclusions:

- *Our data show that overall the beam bridge can hold more weight than the accordion bridge. The median value for the accordion bridge (31 pennies) is less than the median value for the beam bridge (47 pennies).*

- *Even though the data show that the beam bridge "won," we think that the accordion bridge is more reliable. The data for the beam bridge are spread out from 15 pennies to 74 pennies. Most of the accordion bridge data (12 out of 15 trials) are concentrated from 20 to 45 pennies, so you know more about what to expect.*

- *We are glad that we repeated the experiment for each bridge 15 times because fewer trials might have given us a very high or very low number of pennies. It would be interesting to do 50 trials to see what would happen.*

? **What new experiment could Janet and Felix design next to get more information about the strength of bridge designs?**

Comparing Two Sets of Data (page 4 of 4)

Here are two more representations of the bridge data given on pages 80 and 85.

Deon used the letters A and B instead of Xs. This way, he can show the data for both kinds of bridges on one line plot:

Deon's representation

A: Accordion Bridge
B: Beam Bridge

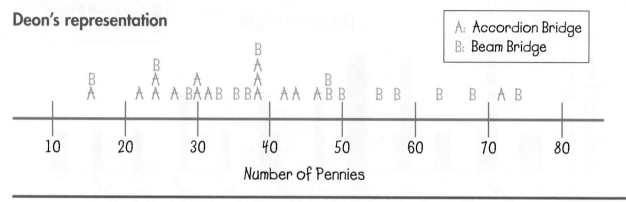

Number of Pennies

Nora made a vertical representation that shows the different bridge types on the left and right sides. Each block represents 1 trial.

Nora's representation

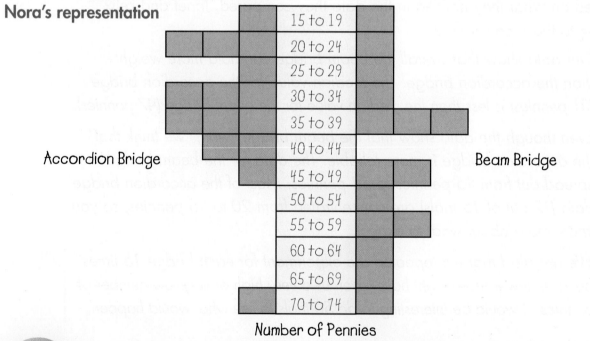

Accordion Bridge | Beam Bridge

| 15 to 19 |
| 20 to 24 |
| 25 to 29 |
| 30 to 34 |
| 35 to 39 |
| 40 to 44 |
| 45 to 49 |
| 50 to 54 |
| 55 to 59 |
| 60 to 64 |
| 65 to 69 |
| 70 to 74 |

Number of Pennies

From looking at these representations what do you notice about the differences between the two kinds of bridges? Which of the four representations on pages 86–88 is the most clear for you?

Probability (page 1 of 3)

Math Words
• probability
• certain
• impossible

How likely is it . . . ? What are the chances . . . ?

Probability is the study of measuring how likely it is that something will happen. Sometimes we estimate probability based on data and experience about how the world works.

Some future events are impossible, based on what we know about the world.

The entire Pacific Ocean will freeze this winter.

Some future events are certain.

The sun will rise tomorrow.

The probability of many other events falls between impossible and certain.

No one in our class will be absent tomorrow.

It will rain next weekend.

Likelihood Line

Impossible		Maybe		Certain
	A		B	

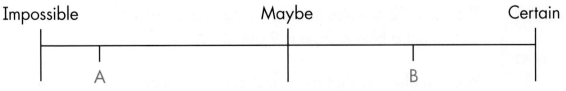

Describe events that can go at points A and B on the Likelihood Line.

Probability (page 2 of 3)

In some situations, there are a certain number of equally likely outcomes. In these situations, you can find the probability of an event by looking at how many different ways it can turn out.

What will happen if you toss a coin?

There are two possible outcomes. You can get heads or tails. If the coin is fair, there is a 1 out of 2 chance that you will get heads and a 1 out of 2 chance that you will get tails.

What will happen if you roll a number cube marked with the numbers 1, 2, 3, 4, 5, and 6?

There are six possible outcomes. If the number cube is fair, all of the outcomes are equally likely.

The probability of rolling a five is 1 out of 6.

What is the chance of rolling an even number?

1	2
3	4
5	6

There are 3 even numbers out of 6 possibilities. So, there is a 3 out of 6 chance of rolling an even number.

You can also say that this is a 1 out of 2 chance.

What will happen if you pull a marble out of a jar that contains 3 yellow marbles and 9 blue marbles?

There are 12 marbles in the jar. The chance of pulling out a blue marble is 9 out of 12.

You can also say that this is a 3 out of 4 chance.

Probability (page 3 of 3)

In mathematics, you can use numbers from 0 to 1 to describe the probability of an event.

The probability of an impossible event is 0.

The probability of a certain event is 1.

The probability of an event that is equally likely to happen or not happen is $\frac{1}{2}$.

For example, when you flip a fair coin there is a 1 out of 2 chance that you will get heads. The probability of getting heads is $\frac{1}{2}$.

Probabilities can fall anywhere from 0 to 1.

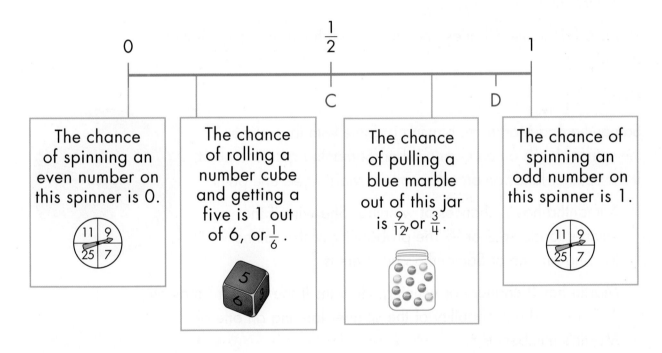

The chance of spinning an even number on this spinner is 0.

The chance of rolling a number cube and getting a five is 1 out of 6, or $\frac{1}{6}$.

The chance of pulling a blue marble out of this jar is $\frac{9}{12}$ or $\frac{3}{4}$.

The chance of spinning an odd number on this spinner is 1.

Describe events that can go at points C and D on the line. You can use the idea of a spinner, a number cube, or pulling marbles out of a jar.

Is This Game Fair?

Math Words
• fair

A game is fair if each player has an equal chance of winning.

Look at these two games.

Game 1

Charles and Hana are playing a game with this spinner. If the spinner lands on an even number, Charles gets one point. If the spinner lands on an odd number, Hana gets one point.

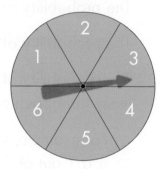

Charles has 3 chances of winning. He wins if the spinner lands on 2, 4, or 6. The probability of the spinner landing on one of Charles' numbers is $\frac{3}{6}$, or $\frac{1}{2}$.

Hana also has 3 chances of winning. She wins if the spinner lands on 1, 3, or 5. The probability of the spinner landing on one of Hana's numbers is also $\frac{3}{6}$, or $\frac{1}{2}$.

This is a fair game. Charles and Hana each have an equal chance of winning.

Game 2

Samantha and Martin are playing a game with this spinner. If the spinner lands on an even number, Samantha gets one point. If the spinner lands on an odd number, Martin gets one point.

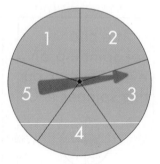

Samantha has 2 chances of winning. She wins if the spinner lands on 2 or 4. The probability of the spinner landing on one of Samantha's numbers is $\frac{2}{5}$.

Martin has 3 chances of winning. He wins if the spinner lands on 1, 3, or 5. The probability of the spinner landing on one of Martin's numbers is $\frac{3}{5}$.

This is not a fair game. Martin's chance of winning is greater than Samantha's chance of winning.

Design a new spinner and describe the scoring rules so that when 3 people play the game, each player has an equal chance of winning.

Polygons

Polygons are closed two-dimensional (2-D) figures with straight sides.

Math Words
• **polygon**
• **two-dimensional (2-D)**

These figures are polygons.

These figures are not polygons.

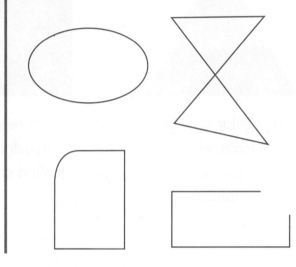

Polygons are named for the number of sides they have.

3 sides	triangle	8 sides	octagon
4 sides	quadrilateral	9 sides	nonagon
5 sides	pentagon	10 sides	decagon
6 sides	hexagon	11 sides	hendecagon
7 sides	heptagon (or septagon)	12 sides	dodecagon

?

What is the name of each of these polygons?

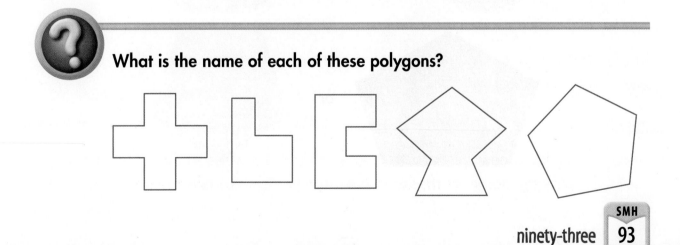

Regular Polygons

Polygons that have equal sides and equal angles are called regular polygons.

a regular triangle
(called an
equilateral
triangle)

a regular
quadrilateral
(called a square)

a regular
hexagon

**Which of these figures are regular polygons?
How do you know?**

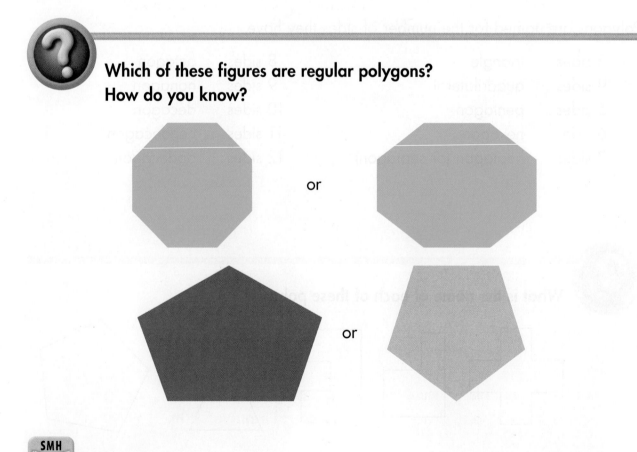

or

or

Triangles

A triangle is a polygon that has:

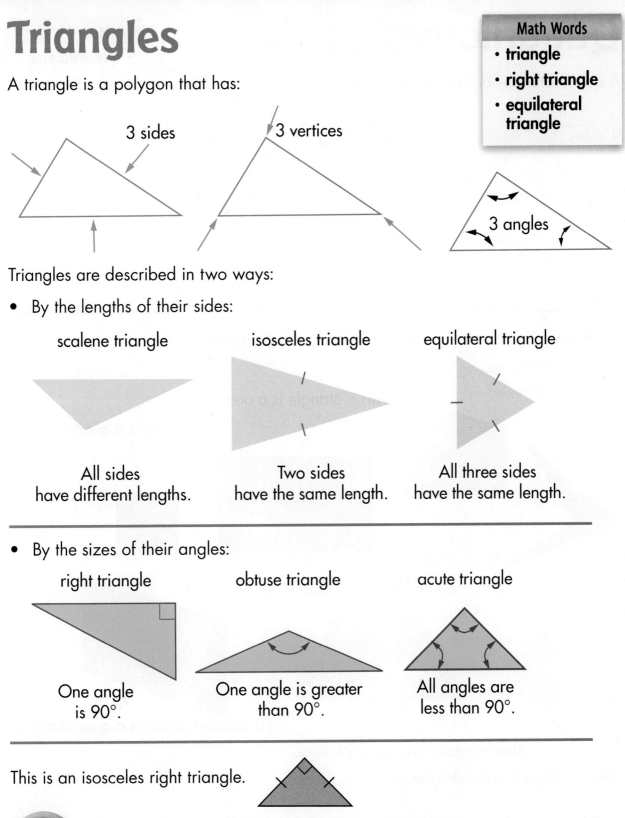

3 sides   3 vertices   3 angles

Triangles are described in two ways:

- By the lengths of their sides:

scalene triangle   isosceles triangle   equilateral triangle

All sides
have different lengths.   Two sides
have the same length.   All three sides
have the same length.

- By the sizes of their angles:

right triangle   obtuse triangle   acute triangle

One angle
is 90°.   One angle is greater
than 90°.   All angles are
less than 90°.

This is an isosceles right triangle.

Draw a scalene acute triangle. Draw an obtuse isosceles triangle. Is it possible to draw a right equilateral triangle? Why or why not?

Quadrilaterals (page 1 of 3)

Math Words
• **quadrilateral**

A quadrilateral is a polygon that has:

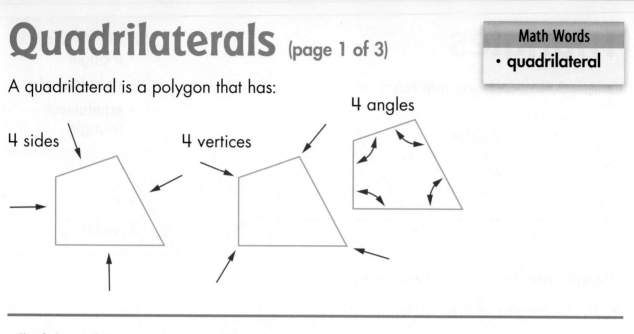

4 sides   4 vertices   4 angles

All of these figures are quadrilaterals. Some quadrilaterals have special names.

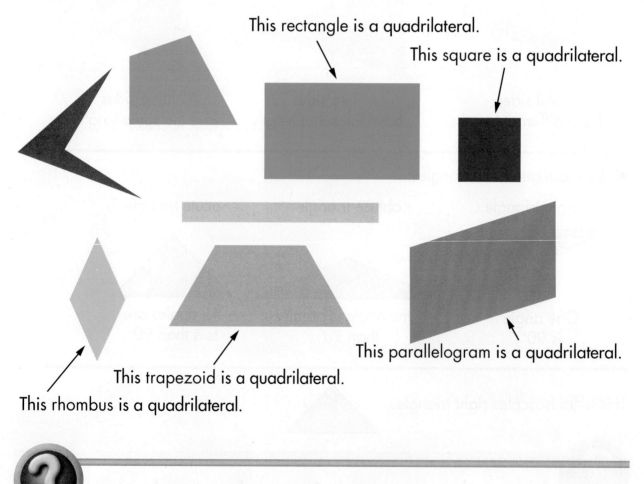

This rectangle is a quadrilateral.

This square is a quadrilateral.

This parallelogram is a quadrilateral.

This trapezoid is a quadrilateral.

This rhombus is a quadrilateral.

Draw a polygon that is a quadrilateral.
Draw a polygon that is not a quadrilateral.

Quadrilaterals (page 2 of 3)

Parallel lines go in the same direction. They run equidistant from one another, like railroad tracks.

Quadrilaterals that have only 1 pair of parallel sides are called trapezoids. Both of these quadrilaterals are trapezoids.

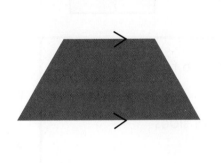

Quadrilaterals that have 2 pairs of parallel sides are called parallelograms. All of these quadrilaterals are parallelograms.

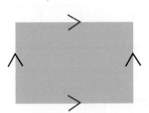

Some quadrilaterals have no parallel sides.

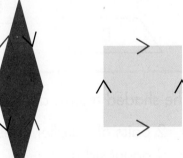

You can use the *LogoPaths* software to draw parallelograms and other polygons.

Quadrilaterals (page 3 of 3)

Some quadrilaterals can be called many different names.

These shaded figures are parallelograms. Each has:

• 2 pairs of parallel sides

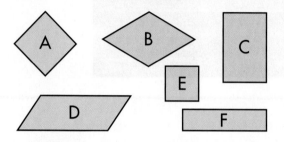

The shaded figures are rectangles. Each has:

• 2 pairs of parallel sides
• 4 right angles

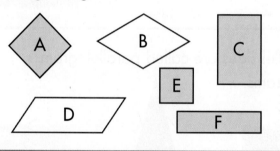

The shaded figures are rhombuses (rhombi). Each has:

• 2 pairs of parallel sides
• 4 equal sides

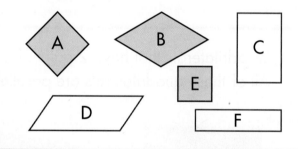

The shaded figures are squares. Each has:

• 2 pairs of parallel sides
• 4 equal sides
• 4 right angles

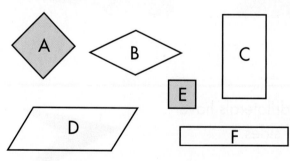

What is the same about rectangles and squares?
What is different about rectangles and squares?

Angles (page 1 of 3)

Math Words
- **angle**
- **degree**
- **right angle**

The measure of an angle in a polygon is the amount of turn between two sides.

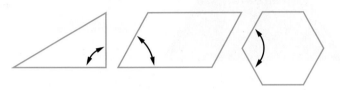

Angles are measured in degrees. When an angle makes a square corner, like the corner of a piece of paper, it is called a right angle. A right angle measures 90 degrees.

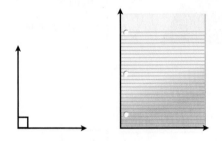

The word *degree* is also a unit that is used to measure temperature.

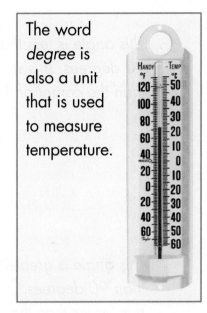

These students are talking about the angles in polygons from their set of Power Polygons™.

Deon: *These triangles all have one 90 degree angle.*

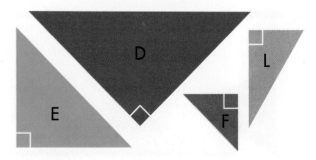

Janet: *All of the angles in all of these rectangles are right angles.*

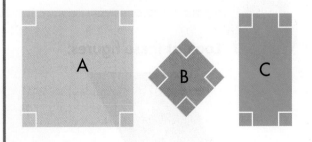

Angles (page 2 of 3)

Math Words
- acute angle
- obtuse angle

Hana: *None of the angles in this trapezoid is 90 degrees.*

This angle is less than 90 degrees. It is smaller than the corner of the paper.

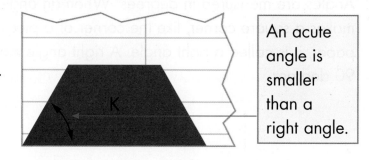

An acute angle is smaller than a right angle.

This angle is greater than 90 degrees. It is larger than the corner of the paper.

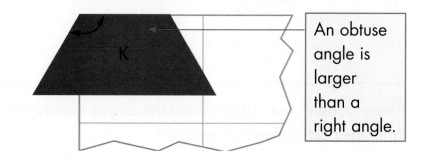

An obtuse angle is larger than a right angle.

Look at these figures:

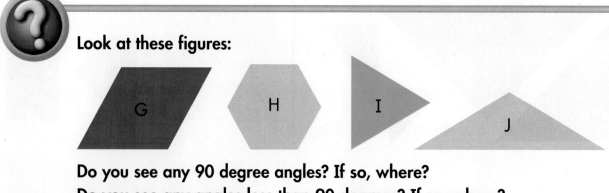

Do you see any 90 degree angles? If so, where?

Do you see any angles less than 90 degrees? If so, where?

Do you see any angles greater than 90 degrees? If so, where?

Angles (page 3 of 3)

How many degrees are in this angle?

How do you know?

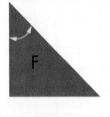

Mitch: I can use two of these triangles to make a square.

45 + 45 = 90

These two angles together make 90°. They are equal, so each angle measures 45°.

How many degrees are in this angle?

How do you know?

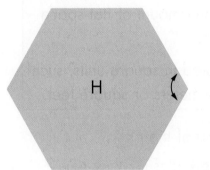

Alicia: When I put three of the hexagons together, three of the angles in the middle make a circle.

360 ÷ 3 = 120

The circle has 360°, so each angle measures 120°.

> You can use the *LogoPaths* software to solve problems about angles.

? **How many degrees are in this angle?**
How do you know?

Perimeter and Area

Math Words
• **perimeter**
• **area**

Lourdes and her father are building a patio. The patio is made up of 1-foot square tiles. They are also building a fence around the patio. Here is a sketch of their patio design.

Lourdes and her father need to use two different measurements for their patio project.

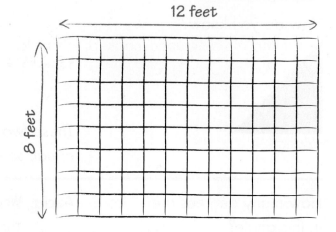

12 feet

8 feet

Perimeter is the length of the border of a figure.

Perimeter is measured in linear units such as centimeters, inches, or feet.

Area is the measure of a 2-D surface, for example the amount of flat space a figure covers.

Area is measured in square units, such as square centimeters or square feet.

What is the perimeter of the patio?

How long will the fence be?

Cecilia:

8 + 12 + 8 + 12 = 40

perimeter = 40 feet

The fence will be **40 feet** long

What is the area of the patio?

How many square tiles do they need?

Mitch:

8 x 12 = 96

Area = 96 square feet

They need **96 tiles**.

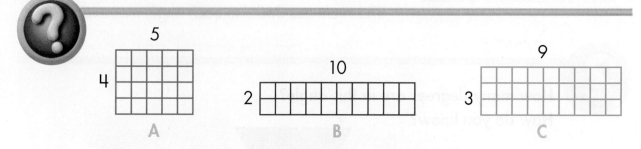

5

4

A

10

2

B

9

3

C

Which two rectangles have the same area?

Which two rectangles have the same perimeter?

Similarity (page 1 of 2)

Math Words
• similar

Two figures are similar if they have exactly the same shape. They do not have to be the same size.

Samantha and Mercedes looked for similar shapes in their set of Power Polygons.

Samantha: *These two triangles are similar.*

They are both isosceles right triangles. Each triangle has one 90° angle and two 45° angles.

The sides of triangle E are twice as long as the corresponding sides of triangle F.

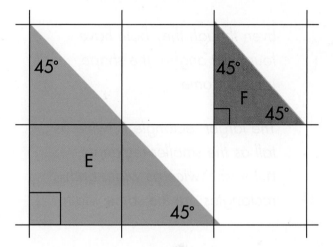

Mercedes: *These two squares are similar.*

They both have four right angles.

The sides of square B are half as long as the corresponding sides of square A.

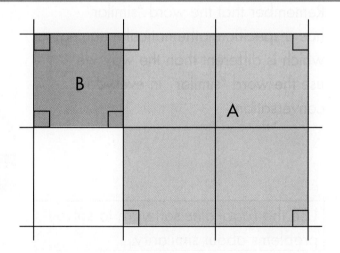

Similarity (page 2 of 2)

Alex compared rectangle C to a rectangle he built using four square B pieces from the Power Polygon set.

Alex: *These two rectangles are NOT similar.*

Even though they both have four right angles, the shape isn't the same.

The larger rectangle is twice as tall as the smaller rectangle, but it isn't twice as wide. Both rectangles are the same width.

Remember that the word "similar" has a specific mathematical meaning, which is different than the way we use the word "similar" in everyday conversation.

Use the *LogoPaths* software to solve problems about similarity.

"Our shirts look similar. We are both wearing stripes."

Draw a rectangle that is similar to rectangle C. How do you know that they are similar?

Rectangular Prisms

Math Words
- **rectangular prism**
- **three-dimensional (3-D)**

A geometric solid is a figure that has three dimensions—length, width, and height.

A rectangular prism is one type of geometric solid. (See other examples of geometric solids on pages 111–114.)

Here are some examples of real-world objects that are shaped like a rectangular prism.

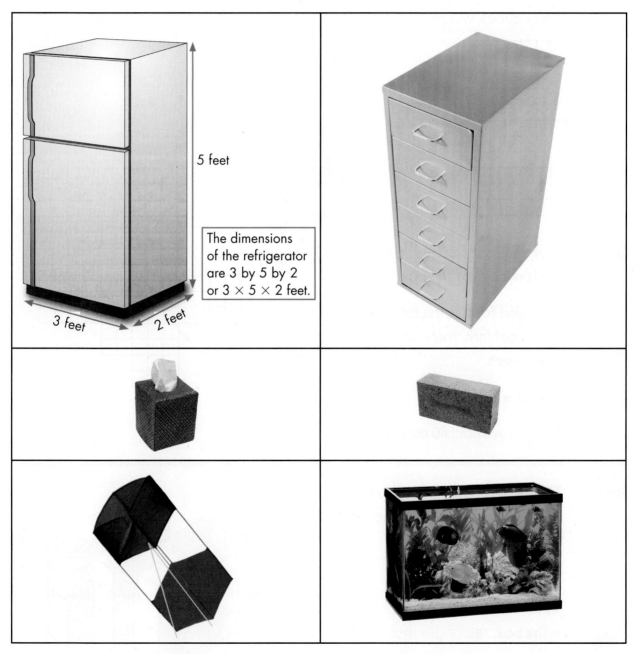

5 feet

The dimensions of the refrigerator are 3 by 5 by 2 or 3 × 5 × 2 feet.

3 feet   2 feet

Volume of Rectangular Prisms (page 1 of 2)

Volume is the amount of space a 3-D object occupies. You can think of the volume of a box as the number of cubes that will completely fill it.

Both Olivia and Joshua solved this problem about the volume of a box.

How many cubes will fit in this box?

Pattern: Picture:

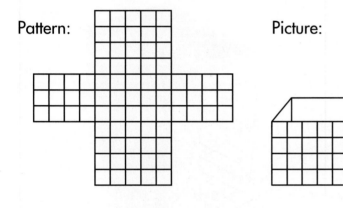

Olivia: There will be 15 cubes on the bottom layer of the box.

When you fold up the sides of the pattern, there will be four layers.

4 x 15 = 60

The box will hold **60 cubes**.

3 x 5 = 15

Joshua: The front of the box is 4 by 5, so there are 20 cubes in the front of the box.

The box goes back 3 slices, so 20, 40, **60 cubes** will fit in the box.

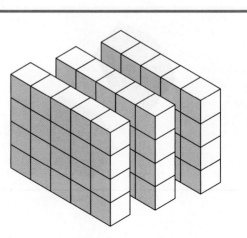

Volume of Rectangular Prisms (page 2 of 2)

Martin solved this problem:

The bottom of a box is 12 units by 5 units. The box is 8 units high. What is the volume of the box?

Martin's solution

The bottom layer of the box will have 60 cubes because 12 x 5 = 60.

12

5 | bottom

Since the box has 8 layers, the total number of cubes is 60 x 8.

So, the volume of the box is **480 cubes**.

$$\begin{array}{r} 60 \\ \times 8 \\ \hline 480 \end{array}$$

Write a strategy for finding the volume of a rectangular prism. Think about how you can determine the number of cubes that fit in a box, whether you start with the box pattern, the picture of a box, or a written description of the box.

Changing the Dimensions and Changing the Volume

Company A and Company B both make identical boxes that have a volume of 6 cubes.

Original Box Design

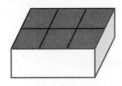

Dimensions: 3 × 2 × 1, holds 6 cubes

Each company has a plan to change the design of the box.

Company A plans to make a box that will hold twice as many cubes.

Company B plans to make a box with double the dimensions.

New Box Design: Company A

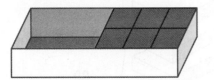

Dimensions: 6 × 2 × 1, holds 12 cubes

New Box Design: Company B

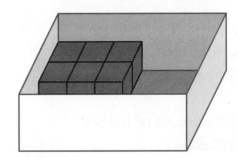

Dimensions: 6 × 4 × 2, holds 48 cubes

Four students discussed how the volume of each new box compares to the volume of the original box.

Company A

Alicia: *The volume of Company A's new box is twice the volume of the original box.*

Olivia: *Only one dimension changed. The 3 doubled to be a 6.*

Company B

Stuart: *Company B's new box will hold 8 times as many cubes as the original box.*

Tavon: *All three of the dimensions were multiplied by 2.*

 Design a different box for Company A that will also hold twice as many cubes as the original 3 × 2 × 1 box.

Standard Cubic Units

(page 1 of 2)

Volume is measured in cubic units.

cubic centimeter	length of an edge	area of a face	volume of the cube
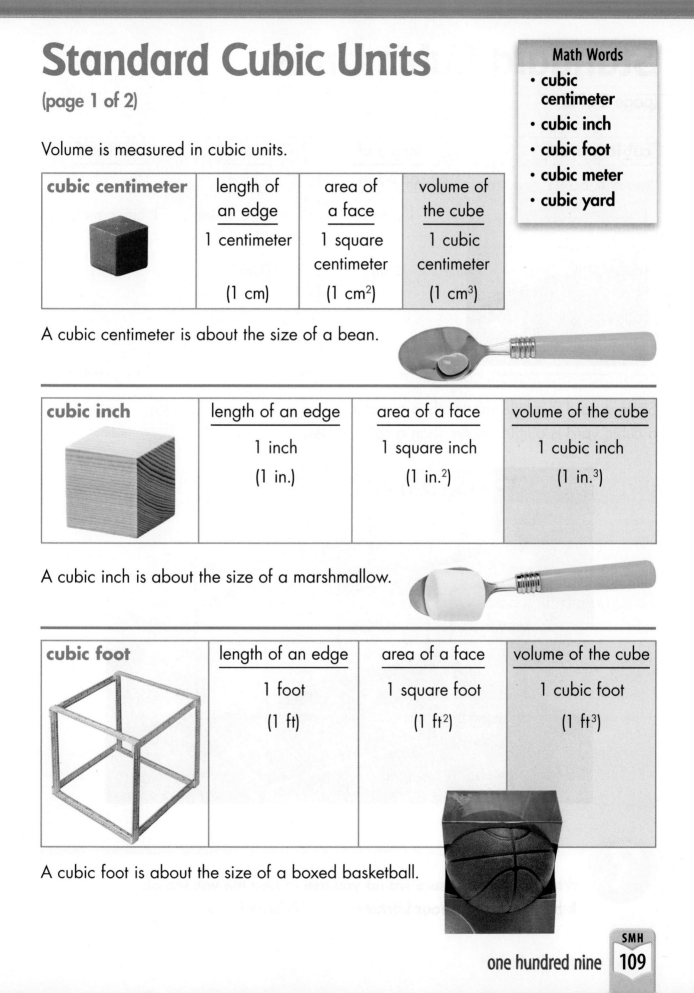	1 centimeter (1 cm)	1 square centimeter (1 cm²)	1 cubic centimeter (1 cm³)

A cubic centimeter is about the size of a bean.

cubic inch	length of an edge	area of a face	volume of the cube
	1 inch (1 in.)	1 square inch (1 in.²)	1 cubic inch (1 in.³)

A cubic inch is about the size of a marshmallow.

cubic foot	length of an edge	area of a face	volume of the cube
	1 foot (1 ft)	1 square foot (1 ft²)	1 cubic foot (1 ft³)

A cubic foot is about the size of a boxed basketball.

Standard Cubic Units

(page 2 of 2)

cubic meter	length of an edge	area of a face	volume of the cube
	1 meter (1 m)	1 square meter (1 m²)	1 cubic meter (1 m³)

Since a yard is a little shorter than a meter,
a cubic yard is a little smaller than a cubic meter.

? Which unit of measure would you use to find the volume of:
A bathtub?   Your kitchen?   A brick?

Geometric Solids (page 1 of 4)

Here are some examples of geometric solids. These figures have three dimensions: length, width, and height.

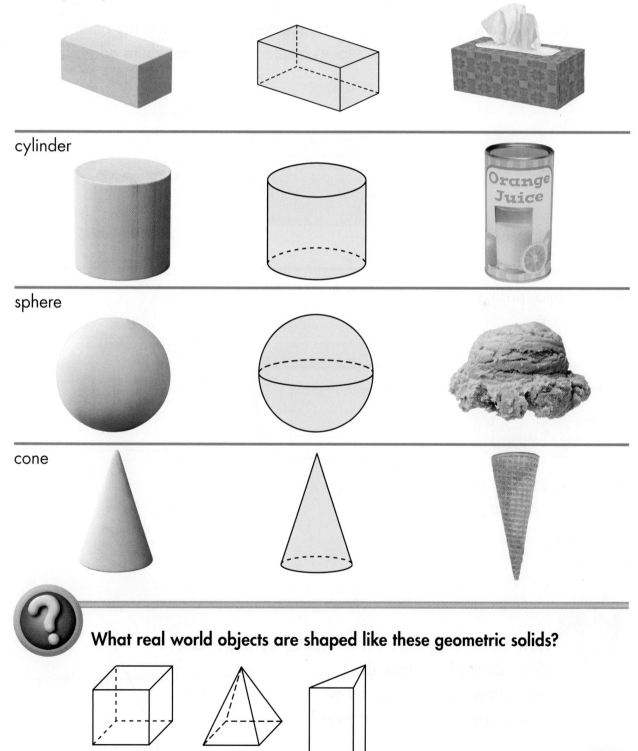

rectangular prism

cylinder

sphere

cone

? **What real world objects are shaped like these geometric solids?**

Geometric Solids (page 2 of 4)

One way to describe a geometric solid is to identify the number of faces, edges, and vertices.

Math Words
- **face**
- **edge**
- **vertex**
- **vertices**

A face is a 2-D figure that makes up a flat surface of a 3-D solid.

An edge is a line segment where two faces meet.

A vertex is the point at a corner where edges meet.

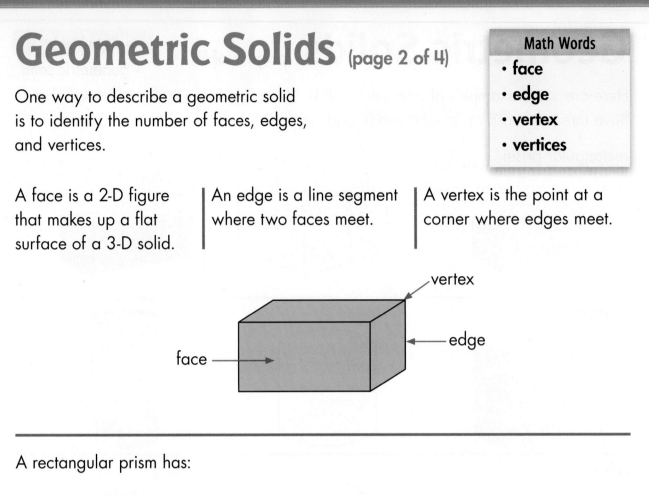

A rectangular prism has:

6 faces

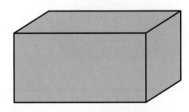

(You cannot see all of the faces in this picture.)

12 edges

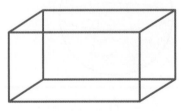

8 vertices

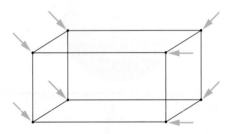

How many faces does this triangular pyramid have?
What do the faces look like?
How many edges does it have?
How many vertices does it have?

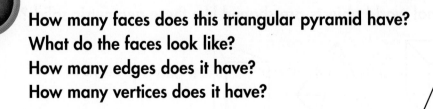

Geometric Solids (page 3 of 4)

All of these geometric solids are called prisms.

The "top" and "bottom" faces
of a prism are called bases.

*The bases of each prism match
one another.*

*The faces on the sides of these
prisms are all rectangles.*

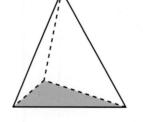
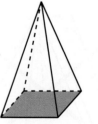
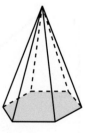

Some prisms, like this one, have faces that are parallelograms
that are not rectangles.

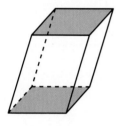

All of these geometric solids are called pyramids.

*The base of each pyramid is
a polygon.*

*There is a point at the top of
each pyramid.*

*The faces on the sides of
the pyramids are all triangles.*

Describe the difference between a prism and a pyramid.

Geometric Solids (page 4 of 4)

The base of this rectangular prism measures 4 centimeters by 5 centimeters.

The base of this rectangular pyramid measures 4 centimeters by 5 centimeters.

The height measures 8 centimeters.

The height measures 8 centimeters.

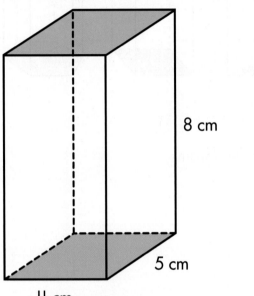

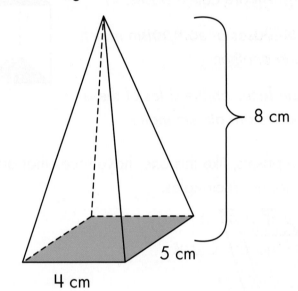

Note: The height of the pyramid is measured vertically from the base, not along the slope of the side.

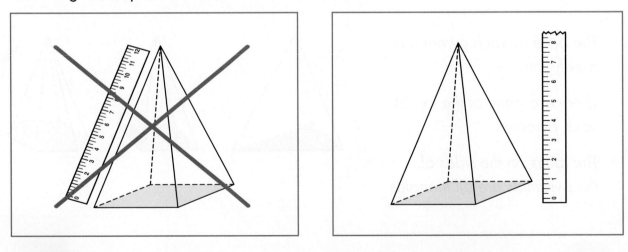

What is the volume of the rectangular prism above?
How do you think the volume of this rectangular pyramid compares
to the volume of the rectangular prism above? How could you find out?

Games Chart

	Use in Unit	Page
Close to 1	6	**G1**
Close to 1,000	3	**G2**
Close to 7,500	3	**G3**
Decimal Double Compare	6	**G4**
Decimals In Between	6	**G5**
Division Compare	1	**G6**
Fill Two	6	**G7**
Fraction Track	4	**G8**
In Between	4	**G10**
Multiplication Compare	1	**G11**
Roll Around the Clock	4	**G12**
Smaller to Larger	6	**G14**

Close to 1

You need

- Decimal Cards, Sets A and B
- *Close to 1* Recording Sheet

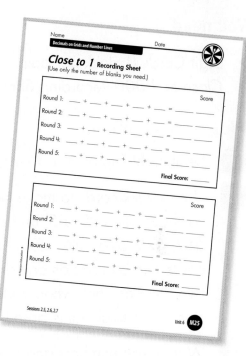

Play with 1 or 2 other players.

The object of the game is to choose cards whose sum is as close to 1 as possible.

 Deal five cards in the middle. Each player uses any or all of these cards to make a total that is as close to 1 as possible. (Everyone uses the same five cards.)

 Write the numbers and the sum on the *Close to 1* Recording Sheet.

 Find your score. The score for the round is the difference between the sum and 1. (Your sum can be under or over 1.)

4 When all players have come up with a sum and a score, compare your results with each other.

5 Put all five cards in the discard pile.

6 Deal five new cards.

7 After five rounds, total your scores. The player with the lowest score wins.

Variations

Follow the rules above, making one or more of these adjustments:

- Make four wild cards to use for play.
- Each player gets his or her own five cards.

Close to 1,000

You need

- Digit Cards (1 deck per pair)
- *Close to 1,000* Recording Sheet

Play with a partner.

1 Deal eight Digit Cards to each player.

2 Use any six cards to make two numbers. For example, a 6, a 5, and a 2 could make 652, 625, 526, 562, 256, or 265. Wild cards can be used as any digit. Try to make two numbers that, when added together, give you a total that is close to 1,000.

3 Write these numbers and their total on the *Close to 1,000* Recording Sheet. For example, 652 + 347 = 999.

4 Find your score. Your score is the difference between your total and 1,000.

5 Put the cards you used in a discard pile. Keep the two cards you did not use for the next round.

6 For the next round, deal six cards to each player. Make more numbers that have a sum close to 1,000.

7 When you run out of cards, mix up the discard pile and use them again.

8 After five rounds, add your scores to find your final score. The player with the lower final score wins.

Variation

Write the score with plus and minus signs to show whether your total is less than or greater than 1,000. For example, if your total is 999, your score is −1. If your total is 1,005, your score is +5. The total of these two scores is +4. Your goal is to get a final score for five rounds that is as close to 0 as possible.

Close to 7,500

You need

- Digit Cards (1 deck per pair)
- *Close to 7,500* Recording Sheet

Play with a partner.

1 Deal ten Digit Cards to each player.

2 Use any seven or eight cards to make two numbers that, when added together, total as close to 7,500 as possible. For example, 3,108 + 4,386 = 7,494 or 7,130 + 372 = 7,502. Wild cards can be used for any digit.

3 Write your numbers and their total on the *Close to 7,500* Recording Sheet.

4 Find your score. Your score is the difference between your total and 7,500.

5 Put the cards you used in the discard pile. Keep the two or three cards you did not use for the next round.

6 For the next round, deal seven or eight new cards to each player (so that each person has ten cards), and play as before.

7 When you run out of cards, mix up the discard pile and use them again.

8 After five rounds, add your scores to find your final score. The player with the lower final score wins.

Variation

Write the score with plus and minus signs to show whether your total is less than or greater than 7,500. For example, if your total is 7,494, your score is −6. If your total is 7,502, your score is +2. Your goal is to get a final score for five rounds that is as close to 0 as possible.

Decimal Double Compare

You need

- Decimal Cards, Set A (2 sets)

Play with a partner.

 Mix the cards and deal them evenly so that each player has the same number of cards. Place the cards facedown in front of you.

 Each player turns over the top two cards in his or her stack.

3 Look at your two numbers and your partner's two numbers. Decide which player has the larger sum.

4 Whoever has the larger sum takes all of the cards that have been turned over and places them at the bottom of his or her stack.

5 If both sums are the same, each player keeps his or her cards. Turn over the next two cards.

6 Play for a given amount of time or until one player has all of the cards. The player with more cards wins.

Variations

Follow the rules above, making one or more of these adjustments:

- The person with the smaller sum takes the cards.
- Include Set B of the Decimal Cards.
- Add new cards. Use either "wild cards" (which could be any number) or "equivalent cards," such as 0.50 or 0.950.

Decimals In Between

You need

- Decimal Cards, Sets A and B

Play with a partner.

 Find the three game cards labeled 0, $\frac{1}{2}$, and 1.
Place these cards on the table (see picture below).

 Mix the Decimal Cards. Deal six to each player.

3 Players take turns placing a card so that it touches another card
in one of these ways:

- to the right of 0
- on either side of $\frac{1}{2}$
- to the left of 1
- on top of any equivalent

As you play a card, read the decimal aloud.

4 Cards must be placed in increasing order, from left to right. A card
may not be placed between two cards that are touching.

0	0.05		0.45	$\frac{1}{2}$		1
zero	five-hundredths		forty-five hundredths	one-half		one

In the example above, the 0.025 card may not be placed between the
0 and 0.05 cards. It cannot be played in this round.

 Your goal is to place as many cards as you can. The round is over when
neither player can place any more cards. Your score is the number of cards
left in your hand.

At the end of the round, the table may look like this:

0	0.05	0.125	0.3	0.4		0.45	$\frac{1}{2}$	0.575	0.65
zero	five-hundredths	one hundred twenty-five thousandths	three-tenths	four-tenths		forty-five hundredths	one-half	five hundred seventy-five thousandths	sixty-five hundredths

0.85	0.925	1
eighty-five hundredths	nine hundred twenty-five thousandths	one

In this sample round, Player 1 could not play 0.25 or 0.6. Player 1 has a score
of 2. Player 2 could not play 0.025. Player 2 has a score of 1.

 At the end of five rounds, the player with the lower score wins.

Division Compare

You need

- Compare Cards (1 deck per pair)

Play with a partner.

1 Divide the deck of cards evenly so that each player has the same number of cards.

2 Each player turns over two cards.

3 Using the larger number as the dividend and the smaller number as the divisor, make a division problem. (For example, if your cards are 80 and 700, the division problem is 700 ÷ 80.)

4 Estimate, compare, and reason about the relationships of the numbers to figure out which player has the greater quotient (answer). Discuss how you know which answer is greater.

5 The person with the greater quotient takes all of the cards. If the quotients are equal, players turn over two new cards and the person with the greater quotient takes all of the cards.

6 Play for a given amount of time or until one player has all of the cards.

Variation

You need

- Digit Cards (1 deck per pair)

Play the same game using Digit Cards with the "0" cards removed. Each player draws five cards. Using the cards in the order they were picked, choose the first three cards to form the dividend and the last two cards to form the divisor. (For example, if you picked 8, 1, 5, 9, 4, your division problem would be 815 ÷ 94.)

Fill Two

You need

- Decimal Cards, Set A (1 set)
- Hundredths Grids for *Fill Two* (1 sheet per player)
- crayons or markers (2 or more colors for each player)

Play with a partner.

1 Mix the cards and turn the deck facedown. Turn over the top four cards and place them faceup in a row.

2 The goal is to shade in two of your grids as completely as possible.

3 Players take turns. On your turn, choose one of the faceup cards, color in that amount on either grid, and write the number below the grid. You may not color in an amount that would more than fill a grid, and you may not split an amount to color in parts of two grids.

4 After one of the four cards has been picked, replace it with the top card from the deck.

5 Change colors for each turn so that you can see the different decimals. As you write the number below each square, use plus (+) signs between the numbers, making an equation that will show the total colored in on each grid.

6 If all of the cards showing are greater than the spaces left on your grids, you lose your turn until a usable card is turned up.

7 The game is over when neither player can choose a card. Players add all of the numbers they have colored in on each grid and then combine those sums to get a final total for both grids. The winner is the player whose final sum is closer to 2.

Variation: *Fill Four*

Follow the rules for *Fill Two* except for the following changes:

- Use Decimal Cards Set A and Set B (1 set of each).
- Each player fills four grids during a game. On a turn, you may color in the amount on any grid that has enough room.
- The winner is the player whose final sum is closer to 4.

Fraction Track (page 1 of 2)

You need

- Fraction Cards
- *Fraction Track* Gameboard
- 20 chips (or other small objects)

**Play with 1 or 2 other players
or in 2 pairs.**

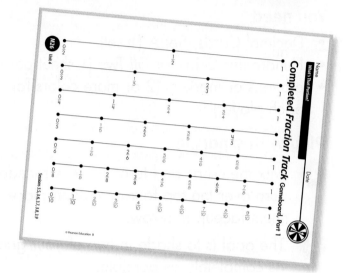

Playing to 1 (Introductory game)

 1 Remove the percent cards and the 18 cards greater than 1 (such as $\frac{3}{2}$) from the deck. Use only Sheet 1 of the *Fraction Track* Gameboard—the part from 0 to 1.

2 Place seven chips on the gameboard, one on each track, at any fraction point less than $\frac{3}{4}$. Mix the cards and place the deck facedown.

3 Players take turns drawing the top card and moving a chip (or chips) to total the amount shown. You can move on one track or on several. For example, if the card is $\frac{3}{5}$, you can move $\frac{3}{5}$ on the fifths line, $\frac{6}{10}$ on the tenths line, or a combination of moves on two or more lines, such as $\frac{1}{2}$ and $\frac{1}{10}$, $\frac{1}{5}$ and $\frac{4}{10}$, or $\frac{1}{3}$, $\frac{1}{6}$, and $\frac{1}{10}$. The fraction on the card is the total that you move chips; it does not indicate points to land on.

Fraction Track (page 2 of 2)

4 The goal is to move chips so that they land exactly on the number 1. When you land on 1, you win the chip. When a chip is won, place a new chip at 0 on the same track so that the next player has a chip on every track. (This happens only when a player has completed a turn. You may not wrap around and keep going on the same track within a turn.)

5 If you are unable to move the total amount of your Fraction Card, you lose your turn.

Playing to 2 (Regular game)

The rules are the same as the introductory version, except for the following:

1 Use all the Fraction Cards and the entire *Fraction Track* Gameboard.

2 The seven chips may be placed on any fractions less than $\frac{3}{2}$.

3 The goal is to move chips so that they land exactly on the number 2.

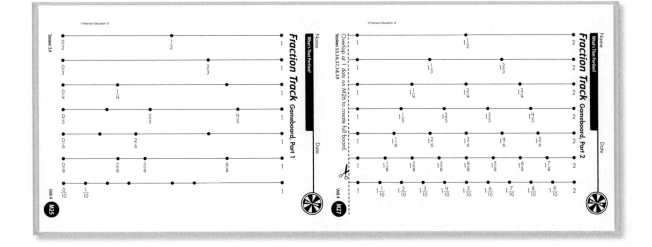

In Between

You need

- Fraction Cards—diamond (◆) cards only
- completed Percent Equivalent Strip (for reference only)

Play with a partner.

 Place the 10%, 50%, and 90% cards on the table (see picture below).

 Mix the Fraction Cards. Deal six to each player.

3 Players take turns placing a card so that it touches another card. You may place a card to the right of 10%, on either side of 50%, to the left of 90%, or on top of any percent. As you play a card, state the fraction and its percent equivalent.

4 Cards must be placed in increasing order, from left to right.

| 10% | $\frac{1}{6}$ | | | $\frac{2}{5}$ | 50% | | | 90% |

A card may *not* be placed between two cards that are touching.

In this example, the $\frac{1}{8}$ card may **not** be placed between the $\frac{1}{6}$ and the 10% cards. So, you cannot place it in this round.

5 Your goal is to place as many cards as you can. The round is over when neither player can place any more cards. Your score is the number of cards left in your hand.

At the end of the round, the table may look like this:

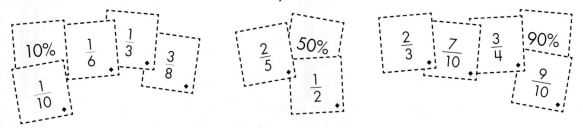

Player 1 could not place $\frac{1}{8}$ and $\frac{4}{5}$ and so has a score of 2.
Player 2 used all six cards and has a score of 0.

6 At the end of five rounds, the player with the lowest score wins.

Multiplication Compare

You need

- Compare Cards (1 deck per pair)

Play with a partner.

 1 Divide the deck of cards evenly so that both players have the same number of cards. Place the cards facedown in a stack in front of you.

2 Each player turns over the top two cards in his or her stack.

3 Determine which player has the greater product. Discuss how you know which product is greater.

4 The person with the greater product takes all of the cards that have been turned over and places them at the bottom of his or her stack.

5 If the products are equal, players turn over two new cards. The person with the greater product takes all of the cards.

 6 Play for a given amount of time or until one player has all of the cards. The player with more cards wins.

Variation

You need

- Digit Cards (1 deck per pair)

Play the same game using Digit Cards with the "0" cards removed. Each player draws 4 cards. Using the cards in the order they were picked, each player forms two 2-digit factors. (For example, if you picked 7, 2, 3, 8, your multiplication problem would be 72 × 38.)

Roll Around the Clock

(page 1 of 2)

You need

- fraction cube, $\frac{1}{2}$ and less
- fraction cube, $\frac{1}{2}$ and greater
- *Clock Fractions* (for reference, from Unit 4)
- copy of the Large Clock Face (for reference)

Play with 1 or 2 other players.

 1 Students alternate who goes first.

2 Choose a fraction cube and roll. Record the fraction. Depending on how close you are to 1, choose a fraction cube and roll again. You may roll up to 3 times.

3 Record the fractions and write an equation to show the sum of all the fractions. You may go over 1. The object of the game is to roll a combination of fractions with a sum closest to 1.

4 The next player takes a turn and rolls up to 3 times. At the end of one round (after each player has rolled), the player who has the sum closest to 1 scores a point. In case of a tie, all players score a point.

Roll Around the Clock

(page 2 of 2)

5 After five rounds, the player with the highest score wins.

Scoring example for one round: Score

Player A $\frac{1}{4} + \frac{7}{12} = \frac{10}{12}$ $1 - \frac{10}{12} = \frac{2}{12}$

Player B $\frac{1}{3} + \frac{3}{4} = \frac{13}{12} = 1\frac{1}{12}$ $1\frac{1}{12} - 1 = \frac{1}{12}$

Player C $\frac{5}{12} + \frac{1}{3} + \frac{5}{12} = \frac{14}{12} = 1\frac{2}{12}$ $1\frac{2}{12} - 1 = \frac{2}{12}$

Player B is closest to 1 and gets 1 point for this round.

Variations:

Positive/Negative Scoring Variation: In a more difficult version of the game, a player's score can be positive or negative. If the player's sum is greater than 1, the score is positive; if the player's sum is less than 1, the score is negative. For example, a sum of $1\frac{1}{12}$ gives a score of $\frac{1}{12}$. If in the next round a player has a sum of $\frac{5}{6}$, the score is $-\frac{1}{6}$. The combined total for the two rounds is $-\frac{1}{12}$. In this version, the winner is the player with the score closest to 0 after several rounds.

Mixed Numbers Variation: Include a number cube for the whole numbers 1 through 6. In this version, players may, if they choose, roll the whole number cube along with a fraction cube. They may not roll the number cube alone. With the numbers rolled, they may add or subtract. Their target answer for this version is 4.

Smaller to Larger

You need

- Decimal Cards, Sets A and B (1 set of each for 2 players,
  2 sets of each for 3 or 4 players)

Play with a partner or in a small group.

 Mix together all of the Decimal Cards.

 Each player draws a 3 × 3 grid for a game mat, with spaces large enough for Decimal Cards to fit inside.

 Mix the combined deck and place it facedown between the players.

4 Players take turns. On your turn, draw the top card from the pile and decide where to place it on your game mat. The numbers must be in increasing order, from left to right in each row and from top to bottom in each column.

5 If you draw a card that you cannot place because of the numbers already on your game mat, you must keep the card in a pile and lose your turn.

Example:
Suppose that after six turns, your game mat looks like this. You draw 0.15 and it cannot be played because 0.375 is already in the lowest place on the board. Put the 0.15 card in your pile of cards that cannot be played.

0.375 three hundred seventy-five thousandths	0.475 four hundred seventy-five thousandths	
	0.55 fifty-five hundredths	0.6 six tenths
0.75 seventy-five hundredths	0.875 eight hundred seventy-five thousandths	

6 If you are unsure which of two numbers is larger, discuss them with other players.

7 The game is over when each player has filled all nine spaces.

8 The winner is the player who has fewer cards that cannot be played. If no player fills all nine spaces of the gameboard, the player with more cards placed on the gameboard is the winner.

Illustrations

6–40, 41–54, 89–90, 108   Thomas Gagliano
40, 75–77, 90   Jeff Grunewald
54, 66   Jared Osterhold

Photographs

Every effort has been made to secure permission and provide appropriate credit for photographic material. The publisher deeply regrets any omission and pledges to correct errors called to its attention in subsequent editions.

Unless otherwise acknowledged, all photographs are the property of Scott Foresman, a division of Pearson Education.

Photo locators denoted as follows: Top (T), Center (C), Bottom (B), Left (L), Right (R), Background (Bkgd)

Cover ©Kris Northern/Phidelity; **41** ©Royalty-Free/Corbis; **79** (TL) ©DK Images, (BR) Blend Images/Getty Images, (TR) Getty Images; **89**© Royalty-Free/Corbis; **97** ©Royalty-Free/Corbis; **105** (TR) Dave Greenwood/ Getty Images, (CL) ©photolibrary/Index Open, (CR) Getty Images, (TL) GK & Vicki Hart/Getty Images; **109** Corbis; **111** (TR, TL)Getty Images